Historical Association Studies

Politics in the Reign of Charles II

To all my former pupils in the Special Subject on
'Charles II and Parliament'

Politics in the Reign of Charles II

K. H. D. HALEY

Basil Blackwell

© K. H. D. Haley 1985

First published 1985

Basil Blackwell Ltd
108 Cowley Road, Oxford OX4 1JF, UK

Basil Blackwell Inc.
432 Park Avenue South, Suite 1505,
New York, NY 10016, USA

British Library Cataloguing in Publication Data

Haley, K.H.D.
    Politics in the reign of Charles II.—
    (Historical Association studies)
    1. Great Britain—Politics and government—1660–1688
    I. Title   II. Series
    320.942   JN201
    ISBN 0–631–13928–1

Library of Congress Cataloging in Publication Data

Haley, Kenneth Harold Dobson.
    Politics in the reign of Charles II.

    (Historical Association Studies)
    Bibliography: p.
    Includes index.
    1. Great Britain—Politics and government—1660–1688. 2. Charles II,
King of England, 1630–1685. I. Title.
DA445.H15   1985   941.06′6   84–28281
ISBN 0–631–13928–1 (pbk.)

Typeset by Cambrian Typesetters, Frimley, Surrey
Printed in Great Britain by Whitstable Litho Ltd, Whitstable, Kent

Contents

Introduction

The politics of the reign of Charles II (1660–85) have never attracted the same attention as those of the previous twenty-five years. This is not to deny that since 1945 a number of important books have appeared; there are biographies of Danby, Shaftesbury and Sunderland, as well as books on the first Whigs and the Popish Plot, on Popery and politics, on the Cavalier House of Commons and on the English public revenue. Yet in quantity they hardly compare with the literature on the 1630s, 1640s and 1650s; there is, for instance, no parallel to the numerous studies of the country communities in the earlier part of the century, other than the occasional chapter in works covering the century as a whole (Evans, 1979; Holmes, 1980). The causes of revolutions and the dramatic events of their unfolding are always more fascinating than the often disillusioning story of their aftermath, with its atmosphere of compromises, calculation and ambition rather than idealism and heroism. The Restoration seems no exception to this rule. The trials of Strafford and Charles I are followed by those of the regicides and the victims of Titus Oates; the ideologies of Levellers and Diggers are succeeded by religious persecution and the irrationality of No-Popery; the battles of Rupert and Cromwell are offset by the ignominy of the Medway; the Long Parliament by the Pensionary Parliament; the romance of Charles II's escape after the battle of Worcester by the intrigues which led to the secret Treaty of Dover with Louis XIV. Everywhere, the superficial story is one of faction, corruption and self-

1

seeking under a king whose essential aim was simply 'not to go on his travels again'.

Yet, on closer inspection, there proves to be much more to it than that. In the first place, the traditional picture of faction, corruption and immorality may have been over-drawn. Historians have recently been emphasizing that there are factions in all periods; no parties, groups or ministries are every totally united, but instead all are to some extent divided in interests, ambitions and ideas about policies to be pursued or the emphasis to be attached to them. For instance, the old tendency to refer to 'Parliament' under the early Stuarts as though it were a monolithic body in rivalry with 'the King' now seems hopelessly simplistic, not to say naive. Circumstances combined to give the impression that the rivalries of Restoration politics were worse than those at other times, but this may to some extent be misleading. Clarendon's account of the period 1660–7 portrays his decline and downfall entirely as the work of a combination of unscrupulous politicians, to whom he never gives credit for any genuine disagreement on matters of policy; but though written in the third person, as though it were the work of an objective historian, it is the work of an embittered statesman defending himself against the accusations which led to his dismissal and banishment. It is natural to feel some sympathy for a man of such public spirit and loyalty to the Stuarts in his second exile, but we should be wary of accepting his portrayal of himself as being, as it were, almost the only man in step in a squad of unruly and badly led rivals for promotion. Again, the unique searchlight of Pepys's diary falls upon the same period and throws much into sharp relief, but it must not be assumed without enquiry that the mind of such an inquisitive, gossiping person, with an eye for his own opportunities as well as the corruption of others, would not have made similar discoveries in another age; its very uniqueness and attractiveness makes the diary a little difficult to keep in proportion. It is also the case that in the reign of Charles II political satire was more prevalent than

2

ever before, in the hands not only of Marvell and Dryden, but of many lesser practitioners. Laughter was as much to the taste of the public as invective; there was a growing number of educated readers, with an ineffective censorship that gave extra spice to the poems of those who evaded it, and who had in the heroic couplet a sharp-edged tool. Politicians as erratic as Buckingham (himself a satirist) or with a record as full of apparent inconsistencies as Shaftesbury were obvious subjects for attack, as well as many lesser figures in a political scene that was relatively circumscribed. It is easy to forget that these were not butterflies, scientifically and objectively mounted, but opponents who were being justly or unjustly pilloried. The poems of the satirists, the diary of Pepys, the coincidence that in this period plays were first written for actresses, and the personal reputation of the king all encouraged a view of the special immorality of the age which, in Victorian times, spread naturally enough to a view of the immorality of its politics. Happy marriages, then as now, existed, but did not make news; nor did some unobtrusive hard work.

The mixture of self-interest and public spirit, which exists in different proportions in all men and at all times, is perhaps particularly easy to study in the Restoration period because men had fewer pretensions and cherished fewer illusions. But the form that political life took was also extremely important in the reign of Charles II. In a sense, a new beginning had to be made after the country had got into a cul-de-sac in which no further progress was possible; yet we must resist the tendency to imagine that in 1660 one book – perhaps that of 'The Early Stuarts' – was closed, and a fresh start was made with 'The Later Stuarts'. No date dividing two periods is ever altogether satisfactory, and 1660 least of all. Both Ogg's book on *England in the Reign of Charles II* (1934) and J. R. Jones's *Country and Court* (1978) avoid it by beginning in 1658, with the disintegration of the Protectorate and Commonwealth. However, it was not simply a matter, to use the metaphor employed by Lord Chancellor Finch in 1675, of the old landmarks reappearing after the floods began to recede. All men's minds were full of the upheavals of the whole period from 1640 to 1660, with its confusions and the impossibility of predicting what even the immediate future would bring or planning for it, with the activities of the soldiers, with the level of taxation (and, by 1660, the trade depression) and with the religious domination of the sects, even though probably more political and social confusion was threatened than actually existed. Long before 1688 the question whether resistance to lawful authority could ever be justified became the most important theoretical problem for contemporaries, and the shibboleth with which Clarendon and Danby hoped to rally a unified Court Party was a test imposing upon all officials and Members of Parliament a declaration of the unlawfulness of resistance and an oath not to endeavour any alteration of the government in Church or State. There was some nostalgia for the successes of the Cromwellian armies and navies against other European powers, but much less for the Cromwellian government in domestic affairs; yet the fear of a Puritan rebellion against the very small forces at the disposal of the ministers of Charles II remained a preoccupation for some years after 1660, and as late as 1681 the most powerful argument of the Tory propagandists was that ''41 is come again' and might, if the Exclusionists were given scope, be followed by 'another '48' (actually January 1649, under the present calendar) and another Commonwealth.

A desire to avoid a return to the instability of the 1640s and 1650s was therefore uppermost in people's minds, but at the same time the Restoration of 1660 was by no means the result of a sweeping Cavalier triumph over crushed Parlimentarians. On the contrary, the Cavaliers had been able to achieve nothing by their own efforts, whether by internal rebellion or with foreign aid. Booth's rebellion in Cheshire in 1659 had been as miserable a failure as Penruddock's in Wiltshire in 1655, and the restoration of the monarchy took place essentially as a result of the disintegration of the army and its inability to find a

4

constructive alternative after the death of Oliver Cromwell. It was a combination of Cavaliers and ex-Parliamentarians that was responsible for the petitions for 'a free Parliament', which greeted General Monck on his march south from Scotland. Even in the early months of 1660 there were some who wished to reach terms for a political and religious settlement before Charles Stuart was allowed to return. They were swept away partly by the violence of the reaction from the Commonwealth and a prudent desire not to alienate the monarch, whose favour would be all-important, but also by Charles's tact in issuing, at Monck's prompting, the Declaration of Breda.

This was, as it were, a policy manifesto, not a treaty, but it seemed to guarantee that Charles would not be vindictive, that there would be no wholesale proscriptions or confiscations of property, that there would be an 'indulgence for tender consciences' rather than a reimposition of Laudian conformity in the Church, and above all a promise to rule in co-operation with Parliament. As with all electoral promises, it remained to be seen how far they were implemented, but the clear implication was that there would be no policy of revenge, no reversal of the concessions which Charles I had made to the Long Parliament in 1641, and no monopoly of patronage for one party rather than another.

Thus, even though there was an overwhelming desire for a return to 'normality' (whatever that was) and a widespread euphoria at Charles's return, and even though, on payment of its arrears of pay and the other promises of the Declaration of Breda, the supposedly Republican army disbanded peacefully (or allowed itself to be shipped off to fight for the Portuguese against the old Spanish enemy), people from widely differing backgrounds had to accept reconciliation or at least peaceful co-existence. Many were united by the common bogey of the Commonwealth, and there was no sharp division of social outlook between Cavaliers and ex-Parliamentarians in the dominant gentry class. A study of the biographies of MPs in the *History of*

5

Parliament (Henning, 1983) shows that, although many families moved from Parliamentarians to Country Party to Whig Exclusionist, or from Cavalier to Court Party to Tory, there were enough who varied from this obvious pattern or who were represented on both sides of the political divide to blur the divisions, to make co-existence easier and to minimize the risk of long-lasting vendettas. In changed circumstances, sons sometimes diverged from the attitudes of their fathers. Nevertheless, the memories of old hostilities were not easily obliterated, and yet everything would have to be done by manipulation, not by the enforcement of a policy by the victors upon the conquered.

If there were differences of background – some Cavaliers had gone into exile, whereas others stayed in England, and Parliamentarians, too, had very different records – there were also differences of personal interest. Research tends to show that not many Cavalier families were ruined by their services to the Royalist cause, composition fees and decimation taxes; but most, more especially those who had spent years in penurious exile without much prospect of returning, felt entitled to some reward for their loyalty and sufferings. After the frustrations of being excluded from advancing their fortunes, they felt entitled to make the most of their opportunities now that 'the sun shone on the other side of the hedge'. Successful pretenders are always called upon to satisfy supporters hungry for their bounty; Charles II, however, was called upon to do this without being able to draw upon resources from the confiscated lands of the defeated, or without being able even to ignore their rival claims to office. It is not difficult to imagine the rivalries of the claimants or the embitterment of the disappointed.

Other problems bred conflicting attitudes during the reign: the question whether an effort should be made to 'comprehend' dissenters within a broad Church of England the question what should be done about the dangers of Popery (particularly when it was associated with the heir to the throne), the question what policy should be adopted towards the expansionist aims of a dominant Louis XIV, with whom James came to be associated. On all these intersecting issues genuine differences of opinion as well as interest were possible.

In these circumstances, political life had to be resumed after an apparently fresh start, following a period in which military force rather than constitutional conventions had been paramount. This, and the striking personalities of Charles and Clarendon, Shaftesbury and Buckingham, James and Arlington, Danby and Halifax, all make the politics of the reign an absorbing subject for study. Underlying all else, however, was the question to what extent government was to be based on consent or on the authority of a hereditary monarch. The issue was never clearly put until Locke published his *Two Treatises of Government* in 1689, drawing on his experience of the reign, much of which was in Shaftesbury's entourage. Charles II did not aim at 'becoming absolute', nor did the House of Commons consciously want to reduce the royal prerogative; the Whigs were neither democrats nor used the term 'the people' in the sense in which it might be used today. For all that, the problem was whether political power should reside in the balanced co-operation of king and Parliament hinted at in the Declaration of Breda, or ultimately in the monarchical authority of the 'Tory reaction' at the end of the reign.

Paradox

Silly History students: crossing out the most important sentences.

D'oh!

1 Politics and the Court

In the reign of Charles II the royal Court was of greater importance than it has been in any reign since. Most political activities were still conducted in the royal palaces – where the king resided day in and day out and was almost always accessible to politicians – rather than in Westminster, where Parliament met for only some months of the year, and not every year at that. In the enlarged Privy Council, which was set up in 1660 (and which met in Whitehall), different points of view were deliberately represented; in any case, virtually anyone of the appropriate social standing could pay his court to his king. It was thought a particular mark of royal disfavour when, in the 1660s, the Earl of Bristol and the Duke of Buckingham were temporarily excluded from the royal presence; one explanation for the plausibility of the Popish Plot was knowledge of the throng of visitors who frequented the palace with only rudimentary 'security precautions'. As for foreign ambassadors, although there was nothing as formal as the levees of Louis XIV, the French, in particular, seem to have visited Whitehall almost daily and to have missed no opportunity, formal or informal, to insinuate their opinions to the king, his brother and his ministers. The ability to play cards or tennis or to engage in courtly conversation were as useful social graces as they had ever been, and we know that sometimes 'casual' exchanges in the queen's room could be turned to account by the skilful just as advantageously as talks held elsewhere in the king's own presence chamber.

I have set out elsewhere some thoughts about the personality of the king (Haley, 1983), and need not restate them here, but a few illustrations may illuminate the way in which a politician's success still depended on the courtier's skill in managing his master. In his *Character of King Charles the Second* (Halifax, 1969, pp. 247–67), Halifax makes clear his technique:

> His ministers were to administer business to him as doctors do physic, wrap it up in something to make it less unpleasant; some skilful digressions were so far from being impertinent that they could not many times fix him to a fair audience without them. His aversion to formality made him dislike a serious discourse, if very long, except it was mixed with something to entertain him.
>
> He walked by his watch, and when he pulled it out to look upon it skilful men would make haste with what they had to say to him.

It was important to be able to tell when Charles was being sincere:

> Those who knew his face fixed their eyes there and thought it more important to see than to hear what he said. His face was as little a blab as most men's, yet though it could not be called a prattling face it would sometimes tell tales to a good observer.

To many, the most important fact about the king was that he was the fount of all bounty, and those who did not ask did not receive, although it was also true that in many cases (though not in the highest political offices) posts were held for life and could not easily be revoked; it was only as the reign proceeded that this practice of giving life tenures was gradually abandoned in some areas. From the very time of his journey from Dover to re-enter his capital in May 1660,

9

he was confronted with the incessant importunities of those who thought that their services to him or to his father entitled them to some recompense, and he was nauseated by this. 'The being galled with importunities, pursued from one room to another with asking faces, the dismal sound of unreasonable complaints and ill-grounded pretences . . . all these would make any man run away from them, and I used to think it was the motive for making him walk so fast' every day in St James's Park. When he was in funds, 'there were those at Court who watched those times as the Spaniards do for the coming in of the Plate Fleet.'

By the end of the reign, when Halifax knew him best, Charles had found ways to 'slide from an asking face', but earlier there were complaints from people such as Sir William Coventry and Sir William Temple that he found it difficult to say no to applicants, and that he made more grants of pensions, concessions and places than a truly economical king would have done. The trouble was that there were not enough rewards to go round. At the Restoration there were places to be given out in the royal bedchamber and household; courtiers with suitable business partners might hope for a share in the farming out of the excise to syndicates; and when the Dutch war broke out in 1665 and subcommissioners for prizes were needed, the thirty names were nearly all those of former Cavaliers (and members of the House of Commons). But it was not politically possible to reserve all the spoils for one victorious party. Many suitors found that the Lord Chamberlain of the new reign was the Earl of Manchester, formerly joined with the five members impeached by Charles I in the Civil War and Parliamentarian commander at Marston Moor, while the mastership of the horse had to be reserved for Monck himself, so that the minor posts in their dependence did not necessarily go to Royalists (it was said that Monck's wife sold them to the highest bidder). Naval posts and commissions tended to go to those with experience under the Commonwealth, or to those who could make use of a powerful patron; amongst these was Samuel Pepys, who at first knew next to nothing about the navy, but was able to make use of the favour of his relative, Edward Montagu, Earl of Sandwich (the naval counterpart of Monck), to gain the Clerkship of the Acts, even though he had to pay £100 from his salary of £350 to the man who claimed the office from pre-Civil War days. Although the royal land sold under the Commonwealth was restored in 1660, there was little enough to give away to any but the most obviously deserving or those who could bring the influence of a powerful courtier to bear; and the pensions and salaries of the places given to the fortunate were often no sooner granted than they fell into arrears in the difficult financial circumstances of the 1660s, aggravated as they were by plague, fire and war and with a totally inadequate system of borrowing at the Crown's disposal.

Of course titles were a cheaper way of giving rewards than grants, which carried with them financial consequences, but the projected new order of the Royal Oak was abandoned and the opening wave of peerages, baronetcies and knighthoods which culminated at the coronation dried up. Charles wisely resolved not to debase his honours by creating more peers for the time being, and was reasonably sparing for the remainder of the reign.

The number of the disappointed, whether their services between 1640 and 1660 were real or exaggerated, was therefore considerable. Local researches by Sir John Habakkuk (1965), Joan Thirsk (1954) and P. G. Holiday (1970), though necessarily incomplete, suggest that most Cavalier families rode out their financial difficulties, but it is easy to see that many thought they had received less than they were entitled to for their services in the Stuarts' hour of need. For this Clarendon rather than Charles received much of the blame. He was accused of not making use of the opportunity at the Restoration to obtain a revenue for the king large enough for him to be as bountiful to his loyal followers as he would have liked. But many who thought that Charles had been favourably disposed to their application for a grant were referred to Clarendon as Lord

11

Chancellor for his consideration and for the legal formalities to be completed, and they complained that they had been obstructed in claims that the king had intended to grant. This was a major reason for Clarendon's unpopularity with the courtiers and contributed to his downfall in 1667.

In this world, ministerial office was an 'office of profit' like any other, and not merely a means of acquiring political power. The Lord Chancellorship and Lord Treasurership were officially worth £8,000 per year, but by income from fees from people who had business with them they were worth considerably more, besides what could be obtained from royal favours and the patronage available to those in a position to make lesser appointments or recommendations on behalf of their relatives and friends. True, they might have to pay some lesser servants, who would nowadays be paid from public funds; on the other hand, direct taxation was very low. It is difficult to work out a modern equivalent for the income from these offices, but one would have to think in terms of annual amounts well into six figures. As for the two secretaries of state, although their salaries were lower, it is a measure of their income from fees that on appointment a new man might have to pay between £6,000 and £10,000 to his predecessor, although sometimes he might receive help from the king or his friends, if his services were wanted badly enough. Before giving up his secretaryship, which was required for Sir Henry Bennet, in 1662 Sir Edward Nicholas asked for, and received, a gift of £10,000 under a privy seal; when, in 1681, the Earl of Sunderland was dismissed for voting for Exclusion against the king's wishes, it was thought a particularly drastic punishment that he was given no reimbursement of the £6,000 that he had paid for the post two years earlier.

There is no space here to enumerate examples of the way in which an office could make a man's personal fortunes or to discuss whether there was any essential difference between what was conventionally permissible in the reign of Charles II, and practices in the earlier reign of, say,

12

James I or the later distribution of the 'loaves and fishes' in the Hanoverian era, except perhaps to make the point that years in exile or in the political wilderness made the matter of reward more urgent for some. We return, however, to the basic point that in the reign of Charles II the source of all places, pensions, titles and power remained, directly or indirectly, the favour of the king and not birth, territorial authority, wealth, landed estates, the wishes of a prime minister or a parliamentary majority. The only exception might be Monck, whose part in the events of 1660 had given him a special claim, but he made no political use of his unrivalled prestige after the Restoration; there were no overpowering magnates and no statesmen imposed upon the king by Parliament. In 1660, it was politically advisable to include a variety of people in the Privy Council, but only the Earl of Bristol was excluded from office by his Catholicism. On the council's all-important committee of foreign affairs, which could discuss whatever business the king thought fit, his choice was unfettered even by any requirement to summon the holder of any particular ministerial office. Few refused office when invited to fill it, although Sir William Temple several times declined a secretaryship of state, and in 1679 the Earl of Essex resigned from his post as First Lord of the Treasury.

The question remains whether Charles allowed his choices to be dictated by others. There can be no doubt that in the scramble for favours and minor office it was useful to have literally 'a friend at Court,' whose influence might procure what otherwise would be inaccessible, but Clarendon thought that Lady Castlemaine's supper-parties amounted to much more than that and that, as turned to their account by his political enemies, they were used to undermine his position. Not only was there what could now be called a significant age-gap between Clarendon, on the one hand, and Charles with his boon-companions, on the other; there was also always a complete antipathy between the Lord Chancellor and 'the Lady', whose name he could not bring himself to mention in his autobiographical account, and he was apt to obstruct the grants that she wanted for herself or her protégés. It all culminated in the famous scene of her triumph in August 1667, when Clarendon left Whitehall after seeing Charles for the last time and she joyfully ran out in her smock to see the old man go.

Suffering severely from gout (or arthritis) to such a degree that he seems to have spent long periods every winter in bed or at least unable to go out, so that the committee of foreign affairs had on occasion to meet in his bedchamber at Worcester House, Clarendon could take little part in the conviviality and suspected the worst of what went on in his absence. He heard, for instance, of the Duke of Buckingham using his powers as a mimic to imitate the Lord Chancellor's ceremonial procession, with the aid of the fire-irons to take the place of his official purse and mace; and not only he, but other contemporary gossip-writers like Pepys, supposed that in 1662 'the Lady' played an important part in the intrigue which replaced Sir Edward Nicholas by her ally Sir Henry Bennet. Yet when events are looked at coolly in retrospect, there were perfectly good political reasons both for the replacement of the aged Nicholas by a man with much greater aptitude for foreign relations, and for the dismissal of Clarendon himself after the failures of the Dutch war, when he was clearly exposed to parliamentary attack. A fresh start was needed from every point of view. On the major issues it is difficult to suppose that Charles took his decisions from anything but a strong sense of what was politically expedient; he never had a true favourite, male or female, and the most that could be said is that the ridicule that people used as a weapon against Clarendon reduced the reluctance he might otherwise have felt to get rid of a minister with such a record of loyal service.

There was one politician who occupied a somewhat unique position at Charles's court. This was the Duke of Buckingham, the son of the murdered favourite of Charles I, who had afterwards arranged for him and the Prince of

14

Wales to be brought up together. Moreover, it was later said that as a young man the duke was responsible for initiating the king into ways of debauchery in exile in Paris. An intimacy dating back to the nursery and fostered by the duke's undoubted qualities as an amusing and entertaining companion enabled him for a long time to survive what would otherwise have been the obvious consequences of his highly erratic political behaviour. After a spell in disgrace for encouraging opposition in the House of Commons and for alleged treasonable practices, including casting the king's horoscope, he was yet within twelve months regarded by some as the king's principal minister after Clarendon's fall. Although he was never given any important office or administrative duties, and fell out of favour with the collapse of the Cabal in 1673, the news that, following a spell in the Tower in 1677, he had again been welcomed back at Court caused the Earl of Danby some dismay. Nevertheless Buckingham could never rely on getting into power his own candidates for the places from which he strove to evict the 'ex-Clarendonians'. In the negotiations leading to the Treaty of Dover he was both duped and manipulated by Charles, who preferred in the last resort to rely on the more solid services of the rival Arlington, who would suppress his own preferences to carry out the royal policy. He used Buckingham, rather than allowing himself to be dominated by him, and in 1677 Danby's fears proved groundless.

Arlington was well-known not only as a subtle courtier, but as a man who 'obliged his friends'. Among his protégés were men as unlike as Sir Thomas Clifford, Sir William Temple, and his under-secretary, Sir Joseph Williamson, who all received advancement through him. But in addition to those whom he helped because of their abilities, it was also at his house at Euston that the famous mock marriage was carried out in 1671 between his master and Louise de Kéroualle, later Duchess of Portsmouth.

Charles had met her for the first time in the entourage of his sister Henrietta at Dover in 1670, and she was widely regarded by Englishmen and the French ambassadors as a representative of France at the English Court. Nevertheless, Charles's preferences for a French alliance were of much longer standing and the most that could be said was that she reinforced them; nor could she prevent him from agreeing to the marriage of William and Mary in 1677. In the concluding years of the reign she was certainly a factor in everyone's political calculations, and when publicly presented to a grand jury as a prostitute and fearful of attack by Shaftesbury and the opposition, it was significant that she was thought to favour Exclusion; but in the end Charles stood by his brother. She was most influential in 1682 when, aided by Charles's increasing age and indolence – he was only in his fifties, but Elizabeth had been the only English monarch since Edward III to reach sixty – and in the absence of suitable alternative candidates, she was able to arrange the recall of Sunderland to Court and to the secretaryship of state. Sunderland, however, had to give assurances about his conduct and to renounce both his previous vote for the Exclusion Bill and his connection with William of Orange. It would not be easy to show that, under the influence of his dearest 'Fubbs', Charles pursued any policy to which he would not have been inclined in any case, often though the name of the Duchess of Portsmouth does crop up in the political manoeuvrings of the Court in the last three years of the reign.

Sunderland needed to return to office, at the price of recanting his previous policies, because his personal financial problems made the income from salary, fees and an attendant pension indispensable. A financial motive may also be part of the explanation for Arlington's earlier reluctant reversal of the foreign policy that he had advocated in the 1660s. Following his residence at the Spanish court, he had been generally thought of as pro-Spanish, he had married a Dutch wife in 1666 and had been behind the Triple Alliance of 1668, which had sought to restrict Louis XIV's conquests from Spain in the War of Devolution. In the correspondence of Charles's sister,

16

Henrietta, she had at first thought of him as an obstacle to her plan for a close union between Charles and Louis, and the French ambassadors never lost their suspicions of him. But Charles answered for Arlington's willingness to follow whatever policy he laid down and, when it came to the point, he signed the secret Treaty of Dover; it is this signature of the French alliance for which he is best known, rather than any resignation when the Triple Alliance was reversed. After a long period in exile, he needed more time in office to build up his fortunes. It is also true, however, that as a loyal Cavalier – wearing with pride a plaster across his nose to cover the scar from a skirmish in the Civil War – he considered it his duty as a minister, whatever advice he might give, to anticipate the king's wishes and to follow whatever instructions he laid down; and though more modern ministerial practice has been different, it was not necessarily an ignoble idea.

If the passport to office was still the royal favour, if the ministers were firmly the king's ministers and the idea of an opposition 'storming the King's closet' still lay in the future, it did not follow that the privy councillors were either ciphers without views of their own or that they were united themselves in the policies which they recommended and carried out. On the contrary, none of the five periods of the reign – 1660–7, 1667–73, 1673–8, 1678–81 and 1681–5 – was without its sharp disagreements. In part, this was the result of Charles's own attitude. He preferred never to have a favourite as close as Buckingham had been to his father, or a *premier ministre* like Mazarin; for he had, after all, witnessed part of the Frondes in France and knew the dangers. Opposing views were tolerated and even tacitly encouraged within his council, and he made little attempt to impose any common and consistent line upon them. In his early teens, he had had to preside over his council in the west in the concluding stages of the Civil War, when there were conflicting views about the military operations to be pursued. In exile, there were always opposing ideas about the means by which he should seek to recover his throne.

17

When he took a decision, the defeated could always hope that he might reverse it under pressure. Perhaps only in some such way was it possible to keep together his band of exiles.

The compromises of the Restoration only added more opinions to be heeded and balanced against each other. The first period (1660-7) was apparently dominated by the Earl of Clarendon as Lord Chancellor, with his immense prestige, his record of long and loyal service, his experience (which others could not match) of how things were done under the English constitution, and long years in which he had been effectively the king's mentor; he never quite adapted his approach as Charles grew older. But in his autobiographical account Clarendon was at pains to argue that he was never all-powerful, as his enemies claimed. There were disputes about whether the king's bride should be Portuguese or Spanish; Clarendon came out in opposition to the Declaration of Indulgence of December 1662, which other ministers had drafted. Arlington was made secretary against his wishes. Clarendon seems to have been justified in saying that he was never enthusiastic about the war of 1664-7 with the Dutch, which was essentially the policy of others; and there were differences over the question whether the war should be ended by means of a separate peace with the United Provinces or with France. In the midst of war, there were bitter disputes over the policy to be adopted towards the Commons' demands for a ban on the import of fat cattle from Ireland, and complaints, from Sir William Coventry among others, about Clarendon's interference in the administration of all departments. In the end, his enemies rejoiced at Clarendon's downfall, flight and banishment, and then there were more disputes about the eviction of ex-Clarendonians from their posts as well.

The second period of the reign (1667-73) was given a misleading appearance of unity by the coincidence that the initials of five of the ministers (Clifford, Arlington, Buckingham, Ashley and Lauderdale) spelt the word *cabal* or secret council, but apart from the fact that these five were never the only members of the inner committee of foreign affairs or cabinet council, they were never united. All favoured some form of comprehension or toleration for dissenters from the Church of England and backed the Declaration of Indulgence of 1672, but some were concerned for Puritans and some for Catholics; all signed a treaty of alliance with France in December 1670 with a view to renewing the war with the Dutch, but only the first two knew of the earlier treaty with its Catholic clauses, which had been signed at Dover in May. In particular, the ministers were riven by the bitter hostility between Buckingham and Arlington, which Charles had to manipulate for the needs of his negotiation with France. This manipulation has often been regarded as an example of Charles's skill, but the fact that it was necessary was a weakness. After the disintegration of the so-called Cabal and the collapse of his foreign policy in 1673–4, the third period (1673–8) was given more unity than the others by Charles's dependence upon the Earl of Danby both for the management of his finances and for the organized build-up of a Court Party in the House of Commons to provide the extra money that was needed. As far as possible Danby would brook no rivals and it was not easy for courtiers to oppose a policy so much in the court's obvious interest. For a year of two, he had to contend with the presence of Arlington, if only in the reduced place of Lord Chamberlain, and, more important, with the hostility of the king's brother James, Duke of York, who held no ministerial office, but whom no Test Act could evict from Charles's counsels. Neither on foreign policy nor on Danby's pro-Anglican attitudes did their views coincide, and James favoured a dissolution, whereas the Lord Treasurer wished to persist with the existing Parliament.

In the fourth period (1678–81), it might have been thought that the need to resist the Exclusionists would have been an obvious incentive for ministers to hold together. However, not only did Danby and James remain at odds

19

until the former was impeached by the Whigs and sent to the Tower, but for some months Charles adopted Sir William Temple's scheme for a Privy Council of thirty, which included Shaftesbury as Lord President and others like Halifax with their own viewpoints. Charles said that 'they should know nothing' and after the inevitable disagreements, for instance over the dissolution or prorogation of Parliament in 1679, Shaftesbury was again dismissed and others resigned as an indication of their determination to press for the exclusion of James. Even in 1680, however, the council was divided between those who, with varying degrees of cordiality, wished to preserve James's rights to the succession and those like Sunderland and Godolphin, who in the end voted for the Exclusion Bill, if only in the interests of William of Orange.

It may seem as though unity was easiest to achieve in the final period of the reign. The Court had ceased to cater for politicians of every outlook; Whigs no longer resorted there, and with no Parliament to use as a platform, they were exposed to the Rye House Plot prosecutions and the attacks on the borough charters. Yet though the government seemed in full control, Halifax, Sunderland and Laurence Hyde (Earl of Rochester from 1682) were at odds with one another. Halifax was a 'Trimmer' rather than a Tory like Hyde. In 1679 he had abandoned the Country Party to favour a policy of limitations on the power of a Popish successor rather than exclusion; but he was not at ease in a period with no Parliament, with persecution of dissenters and favour to France rather than William of Orange. If James had to acknowledge the services of the opponent of Exclusion, he disliked the supporter of limitations and preferred his brother-in-law Rochester. As for Sunderland, neither in terms of personality nor in terms of his very different record was he likely to work smoothly with either of his rivals, even if James had been willing to trust him. Throughout the reign, therefore, there were acute personal rivalries, but there were also urgent political issues of domestic and foreign policy as well as religion on which it

20

was possible and legitimate to disagree. Charles's attitude was always that it was best to play off one minister against another in the interests of whatever policy seemed expedient at the time. He was not regarded as being either consistent or immune to pressure, but rather as someone who could be influenced in one direction or another by temporary circumstance. He was an opportunist rather than a man pursuing deep schemes 'to make himself absolute' (whatever that might mean). He would use rivalries and events to gain more elbow-room for himself, and in that way there was a trend towards an increase in royal authority.

In this he had the usual assistance of some second-rank administrators. In spite of the period's not unjustified reputation for embezzlement and peculation, particularly in the second Anglo-Dutch war, and in spite of the apparently inefficient system of patronage which recruited them, people like Pepys at the Navy Office and Admiralty, Downing as secretary to the Treasury commissioners from 1667 to 1671, Williamson as under-secretary (and later secretary) of state, Guy as secretary to the Treasury from 1679 to 1689, Blathwayt in a number of posts, Bridgeman as under-secretary of state, Sir Stephen Fox as paymaster to the forces (and later Lord of the Treasury) all helped to make government more methodical and more effective. Of these, none received a peerage like the more eminent politicians of the reign, and Downing's baronetcy was awarded for services other than those to the Treasury; Williamson and Fox received knighthoods and the others no titles. Only Fox can be said to have belonged to the courtiers close to the king; all were his servants and contributed in different ways to the strengthening of the monarchy.

The chief restraint upon the king's authority was Parliament. Care must be taken not to regard the politics of the reign as a continuous, conscious struggle between king and Parliament; Parliament was never a monolithic body, and contained many dependants of the king within it. But in the last resort, Charles had to rely upon its co-operation

21

to raise money and to pass laws; and the House of Commons had always possessed the power and the duty loyally to present and to press the subjects' grievances, and was indeed encouraged to do so by some of the king's own privy councillors for their own purposes, to strengthen their hand in the rivalries at Court.

2   Politics and Parliament

Whereas the royal Court was always in existence, even if at Newmarket it operated on a reduced scale and with no formal meetings of the Privy Council, Parliament sat only intermittently. The Long Parliament had been in almost continuous session from 1640 to 1653, and even in 1660, October had been the only month without a meeting; but from the end of the busy Convention in December 1660, sessions averaged only eleven weeks per year. In 1671–3, 1675–7 and 1679–80, there were intervals of twenty-two, fifteen and seventeen months respectively, and for almost four years at the end of the reign there were no meetings at all, in spite of the provisions of the Triennial Acts. Although eventually the growing infrequency caused some dissatisfaction and a demand for annual Parliaments, it was recognized on all sides that it was within the king's power to call, prorogue or dissolve Parliaments as he chose; adjournments came to cause some dispute.

On average the meetings lasted no longer than the summer recess nowadays, but while they lasted Parliament tended to monopolize the attention of ministers and even, as the reign proceeded, of foreign ambassadors who detected its influence upon policy. The year 1660 has been described as a restoration of Parliament as well as a restoration of the king. For twenty years beforehand there had been no Parliament that had not existed under the shadow of the soldiers, whether of Charles I or of Cromwell; there had been no free elections, and indeed no Parliament whose members had not been purged or even finally evicted by military force (except for Barebones' Parliament, which 'proves the rule' because its members were nominated by the Army Council). The Restoration made possible a resumption of normal parliamentary life without the threatening shadow of a *coup d'état*, although in 1667, 1673 and 1678 the raising of troops for the government's foreign wars still caused some suspicions that they might be used against the king's own subjects. Certainly, at the beginning of the reign, the Declaration of Breda implied that Charles would pay heed to the advice of Parliament, although no member expected that its infrequent meetings would exercise anything like day-to-day control. Only time would show that even a body of Cavaliers would almost inevitably develop a tendency to criticize, and that the king's relations with it would not run smoothly.

Except in the 1650s, the word 'Parliament' in the seventeenth century can never be used as though it were simply an equivalent for 'the House of Commons', and it is necessary to begin by saying something about the constitutional position and attitudes of the House of Lords. The peers were the more assertive because the House had been abolished in 1649 as being 'useless and dangerous'. When the lay peers were restored to the Convention, followed by the bishops in 1661, those people who wanted to get back to the traditional constitution regarded them as a necessary part of the social and political hierarchy and as a bulwark against another revolutionary outbreak. Even under the Commonwealth the peers had retained their titles; they were not reduced, like the aristocracy in the times of the French Revolution, to be 'Citizen Cecil', 'Citizen Cavendish' or 'Citizen Percy'. Although Charles restricted the giving of new titles after his coronation, his principal ministers received them as a matter of course. Even Halifax, who regarded titles as 'rattles', said 'that since the world were such fools as to value these matters, a man must be a fool for company', and accepted not only a peerage but two promotions within it. Shaftesbury's patronage of radicals and dissenters did not prevent him from putting a

24

high value on the place of the nobility in the constitution. It is worth noticing that of Charles's leading ministers only Clifford, Sir Thomas Osborne (Earl of Danby) and Laurence Hyde (Earl of Rochester) spent an appreciable period in the Commons before being promoted to the Upper House. Clarendon, Arlington, Shaftesbury (longer a royal minister than an opposition leader) and Halifax each sat in the Lower House in a maximum of four different years; Buckingham, Sunderland, Ormonde, Essex and Lauderdale (as well as the Duke of York) not at all.

The House of Lords thus contained the most experienced statesmen, but even its lesser members were not prepared tamely to follow whatever policy lead the House of Commons gave, and they were extremely sensitive to anything which could be deemed to affect their privileges. This was the time when they asserted themselves as the highest court of appeal from the common law courts; and in the case of *Skinner* v. *The East India Company* they even tried (although in the end they had effectively to abandon their claim) to set themselves up as a court of first instance in cases where no other court had jurisdiction. Several times a deadlock developed in disputes with the House of Commons, leading to conferences between 'managers' of the two Houses or free conferences to which any member could go. When no agreement could be reached and the deadlock could not be broken, as for instance over *Shirley* v. *Fagg* in 1675, there was no alternative but to bring the session to an end. For politicians who for some reason wanted to bring the session to an end – or even for Charles – it was an obvious tactic to try to bring about such a deadlock by getting passions roused in either House and relying on the natural propensity of each to stand up for what it believed to be its rights.

Obviously this was most important in the case of legislation, which required the consent of both Houses. Bills such as the *Habeas Corpus* Bill had to be introduced in several sessions before they were passed, and some, most notably the Exclusion Bill of 1680, were never passed. The

25

Lords' rejection of it was decisive, and the Exclusionist majority in the Commons (where the Court Party had not even dared to call for a vote) was powerless against it. The possibilities of obstruction were almost endless, and Charles could exploit this to fend off Bills that were inconvenient. Not only did the House of Lords contain many ministers and courtiers, including some whose titles had been granted as rewards for recent and loyal service; there also were the bishops who had been nominated by the king. Charles's choices of bishops were always respectable ones, and they were not mere stooges; but after the Civil War the interests of the Crown and the Church were so obviously allied that normally almost all the bishops could be relied upon to vote as the king wanted. There were twenty-six bishops, and in a house with a normal attendance of less than a hundred, even though proxies could also be counted, their vote with the court was difficult to defeat. In 1675 Shaftesbury rudely described them as 'the dead weight', because, however open other peers might be to argument, there was no means of moving the bishops.

The king also had one other way of exercising influence upon the peers. In 1670, he revived the old practice of informally attending debates in the Lords himself, even saying that it was better than going to the play. One has to imagine Charles standing near to the fire, making interjections to influence doubtful peers, or engaging in whispered consultations with his ministers. This was most important at the time of the rejection of the Exclusion Bill on its first reading in the Lords in 1680, when his presence disposed of any rumours that he might be brought to favour it.

If the Lords could be relied upon to block the more inconvenient Bills sent up by the Commons, they could however do little to help the king to gain what became his most important objective in calling Parliament, namely further supplies of money. In 1671, they did try to amend a Commons Bill to vary the rate on sugar, a matter on which colonial planters, refiners and shippers had different interests, but this only led to uproar, deadlock, the end of the session and the loss of the money Bill altogether. It was noticed that ministers took different sides in the dispute, but this may not have been entirely factious; for the money Bill also contained a ban on the import of French brandy, which it would have been difficult for ministers either to oppose, because it was so strongly desired by the Commons, or to defend to Louis XIV, with whom Charles then had his secret alliance.

Even the Cavalier House of Commons insisted on retaining control over the voting of taxation, and there are scattered remarks to be found from individual members complaining, for instance, that the new hearth tax of 1662, the likely yield of which was wildly exaggerated, would make it unnecessary for Charles to meet his Parliament regularly. Originally, however, it seems improbable that the House wanted deliberately to give the king a revenue that was inadequate. Certainly taxation would need to be defended to constituents, and the Commonwealth had ended with a serious depression, which made it desirable to seek relief from the wartime burden; but the new regime had to be maintained against possible rebellion and many members hoped to profit themselves from the royal bounty. Professor Chandaman (1975) plausibly contends that with good financial management the revenue could have been made adequate; but this good financial management was not immediately received, and appeals for additional taxation succeeded one another in most sessions.

The House of Commons to which these appeals were made was the old unreformed House of pre-Civil War days, already known to include the rotten boroughs and the haphazard local franchises that lasted down to the Reform Bill of 1832. All the demands of the Levellers for a more democratic or more rational system of representation faded away, identified with civil war and social disorder, and were not explicitly revived even in the agitation of 1678–81, although there were demands for annual Parliaments and for action against bribery in elections. In the 1670s the county and city of Durham gained seats for the first time, and Charles II created one new parliamentary borough at Newark; but this revival of the old royal power to bring new seats into existence created fears amongst the opposition and it was not tried again even in the Tory reaction of the 1680s. Of course there were people who realized how logically indefensible the system was even a century and a half before 1832. Among these was Sir William Petty, one of the earliest exponents of 'political arithmetic', or the application of statistics to politics – although like many statistics, particularly in round numbers, his are no better than well-informed guesses.

In a memorandum which Petty drew up for his own use he calculated that the total electorate was under 200,000 (Browning, 1953, pp. 216–17). This appears to have been an underestimate, because the numbers of voters for each constituency given in the first volume of the *History of Parliament* (Henning, 1983) for the years 1660–9 total over 234,000. (The number has to be given in this way, because in the more open constituencies the only figure that can be given is of those who actually voted at an election, not those entitled to vote.) It seems safe to assume that the electorate in fact totalled upwards of 300,000, and that this might have equalled 20–25 per cent of the adult male population. Petty further estimated that the elections were 'governed by less than 2,000 active men', which would have made an average of only eight per constituency; it is not clear precisely what he meant by 'active men', but by this small number he may have intended to indicate those men of influence who decided whose name should go forward for an election. He said that out of the 211 borough constituencies there were ten (London, Westminster, Southwark, York, Newcastle, Exeter, Bristol, Canterbury, Coventry and Chester) which he estimated to be worth double all the remaining 201; he remarked that Cornwall sent ten times as many members as Cheshire, and that the franchise varied from borough to borough. His final comment was that 'there is nothing more odious and grievous in the dispensation of authorities . . . than inequality.' In modern eyes he

28

was right, but the great majority of his contemporaries did not see it in this way. After what had happened in 1640–60 they saw the best safeguard for social and constitutional stability in the preservation of traditional rights.

The practical result was that the House of Commons was heavily dominated by the country gentry. There were many more borough than county seats, but only 173 members are listed as merchants and 277 as lawyers, out of 2,000 members in the period 1660–90; the boroughs looked overwhelmingly to the nearby county families. This was reflected in members' attitudes: for instance, in their reluctance to impose a land-tax, which did not become a regular tax until 1692; in the corn laws of 1663; and in the Irish Cattle Act of 1667, which protected English land-owners, led by the members for the heavily over-represented counties of the south-west, against the competition of fat cattle imported from Ireland. The Game Act of 1671 laid it down that no one who did not possess land worth £100 per annum was allowed to own any 'guns, bows, greyhounds, setting-dogs, ferrets, cony-dogs, lurchers, hays, nets, low-bells, hare-pipes, snares or other engines', and the lord of the manor's gamekeeper, armed with a warrant from his master or a fellow justice of the peace, could search for them and seize or destroy them as poaching equipment.

Clarendon told the Cavalier Parliament when it assembled in 1661 (and none of his hearers would have contradicted him) that:

> no man undervalues the common people of England, who are in truth the best and the honestest, aye, and the wisest common people in the world, when he says they are not fit to model the government they are to live under, or to make the laws they are to obey. . . . It is the privilege . . . of the common people of England to be represented by the greatest and learnedest and wealthiest and wisest persons that can be chose out of the nation; and the confounding the commons of England, which is a noble representative . . . with the

29

common people of England was the first ingredient into that accursed dose, which intoxicated the brains of men with that imagination of a commonwealth. (*Parliamentary History*, 1806–20, iv. 206)

The moral was clear that in a monarchy all should be content to be represented by their social superiors. There are qualifications to be made to this picture of gentry dominance, however. There was no sharp line to be drawn between landowners and townspeople. Country squires had their interests in trade, and were well aware of the extent to which the national interest, and often the particular interest of the boroughs which they represented, depended upon it; this underlay both the Commons' pressure for war against the Dutch in 1664, and the later preference for Spain rather than France, with whom England had an unfavourable balance of trade and where it had to contend with Colbert's protectionist policy. Moreover, the members had to come to Westminster for their meetings (apart from two short sessions at Oxford) and were near enough to the City of London itself to be quite unable to assemble insulated from public opinion, as we shall see in the next chapter. The size of the House, with its 513 members, unlike the 36 members of the Castilian Cortes, meant that it could never become a small clique.

The procedures of the House of Commons were already fairly well developed. There were clearly established stages in the legislative process, with different readings and so on; the convention had grown up that all money Bills had to be discussed in a grand committee of the whole House; members had learned to fight their parliamentary battles in terms of the rules and precedents and under the chairmanship of the Speaker (who was still, until 1679 at least, in effect a government nominee with an official salary as well as fees for private Bills). Some meetings were more unruly than others, but, considering the heat some issues engendered and the general reputation of Englishmen for turbulence, there was less disorder than might have been expected. There were one or two scuffles in the lobbies, and meetings of committees might be more disorderly than sittings of the House. Pepys commented unfavourably upon the committees before which he appeared and there was one occasion when swords were almost drawn; it was claimed 'that Lord Cavendish spit in Sir John Hanmer's face, but that was only eagerness of speech, and so some might accidentally fly from him'. After nearly half an hour's disorder, the situation was saved when the Speaker took the chair, thus converting the committee into a meeting of the House itself, and order was immediately restored. But this was a very rare case, and the House was plainly ashamed of it (Grey, 1763, iii. 128–9).

In other respects, however, practices were still un-developed and even informal, by modern standards. Many members drifted up slowly some days after the beginning of the session, to such a degree that, as time went on, some who were reluctant to grant supply feared that the courtiers who were present in London would rush it through before there was a full House. They went off into the country before the end of the session, particularly if it was in July: in July 1667, the temper of already discontented members was not improved when they were brought long distances only to be dismissed after three days. When they were in London, they did not always turn up at eight o'clock, when the House was supposed to meet, and they were apt to go off to dinner or the playhouse before the vote was taken. When the Exclusion Bill received its first reading there was a thin House, it was said, because there was a dog match at Hampton Court and a horse match on Banstead Downs (Historical Manuscripts Commission, *Ormonde MSS*, NS v. 102). One freezing February day, when they found on arrival that there was a window broken, they simply adjourned. Members needed leave of absence to go into the country before the session was over, and from time to time there was a roll call, following which those without excuse would be sent for in custody; the very fact that this was necessary, however, suggests that attendance had dropped.

At the biggest division of the reign there were still 142 members who did not vote, and in October–December 1678, in all the excitement of the Popish Plot, on average only half the members voted. The vote on the second reading of the Exclusion Bill of 1679 was the only occasion, so far as I know, when those in favour exceeded 200 (in a House of 513), although it is fair to add that in addition to the 204 who stood up to be counted there is also some evidence of pairing.

In such conditions, it was extremely difficult to control the House, the more because none of the king's principal ministers sat in the Commons after reaching eminence. When the government needed an unprecedentedly large sum of money for the Dutch war in 1664, it did not put up a minister to call for the grant; instead it arranged for a back-bencher named Paston, who would in the eyes of the members have no axe to grind, to make a proposal. He had to wait for his reward until 1673, when he became Viscount Yarmouth (Clarendon, 1827, ii. 303–15). The lesser privy councillors who sat in the Commons were a useful channel of communication, but they never had the authority to dominate debate and had indeed to avoid anything which looked like too blatant interference with members' freedom to reach decisions.

Yet the leading politicians, though they sat in the Lords, found it useful as the 1660s proceeded to cultivate a clientele among the members in the Commons. Clarendon relied on a small group of Cavaliers, who held no major office, to give some guidance to the business of the House; to his dismay some of his enemies, such as Sir William Coventry, obtained entrance to the number with whom he held daily consultations, and the House fell entirely out of control in 1667. Arlington, Buckingham and Danby had their own groups of supporters in the following years, partly because in their rivalries for the king's favour it was useful to claim that they could predict the way in which the House would go and influence its business, and partly as a hedge against the recurring possibility of impeachment by the

Commons which, next to the loss of the royal favour, was the greatest danger that a minister could face. In fact the cumbersome procedure of impeachment was never successful against a royal minister and Danby, in the agitation of the Popish Plot, was the only one who even had to go to the Tower when charged. Addresses asking the king to dismiss ministers from his counsels were no more successful. But the supporters of one minister could intrigue against the position of another and feel sometimes that they were not without encouragement in the circle round the king.

So, as high hopes dwindled in the débâcle of 1667 and high taxation seemed to have been wasted, loose political groupings came into existence and the regular attendance of members became more important. In retrospect, it seems that there was almost bound to be a tendency for the groups to merge into 'government' and 'opposition' supporters, but this (to us) natural development was disapproved by many people, who regarded it as being factious. Amongst them, for instance, was Roger Pepys, a relative of the diarist and member for Cambridge.

> He doth bewail the constitution of this House, and says there is a direct cabal and faction, as much as is possible between those for and those against the Chancellor [Clarendon], and so in other factions, that there is nothing almost done honestly and with integrity; only some few, he says, there are, that do keep out of all plots and combinations, and when their time comes will speak and see right done, if possible. . . . He tells me that he thanks God he never knew what it was to be tempted to be a knave in his life, till he did come into the House of Commons, where there is nothing done but by passion, and faction, and private interest. (Pepys, *Diary*, 31 October 1667)

This might seem to be a commonplace diatribe by a disgruntled member against the House to which he belonged, but it implies a constitutional view in which every issue was debated separately on its merits and in which parliamentary tactics had no place, and as politics became more complex this more and more resembled Canute trying to hold back the tide.

In 1673, when a speaker used the now-familiar phrases 'this side of the House' and 'that side of the House', because people of like political views were sitting together, it was argued that these words were unparliamentary; 'it is against the order.' But this view was getting to be a very old-fashioned one, and realistic observers had to recognize that in a very imprecise way there was something which could be called a 'Court Party' and something which could be called a 'Country Party'. We read without surprise of pre-session gatherings of opposition members in a tavern, and even of some of them abandoning a planned dinner when a session was unexpectedly cut short by a prorogation. In 1675 the secretaries of state sent round a kind of 'whip' before the session to members whose presence was thought to be particularly desirable from the Court point of view (Browning, 1951, i. 171–2; iii. 56–61; Henning, 1940, pp. 128–9).

In whipping up support in the third period of the reign, Danby had important advantages in the patronage at his disposal. He tried to build his 'Court Party' partly on policies designed to appeal to the Cavalier and Anglican prejudices of members, such as the non-resistance test of 1675 and action against Dissenters, and partly by an anti-French foreign policy (when he could persuade the king to agree to it), based on the marriage of the king's niece Mary to William of Orange in 1677. But he also used the important fact, which he was not the first to recognize, that there were up to a hundred members who had some kind of minor office, pensions or dependence upon court and might be the nucleus of a 'Court Party'. They would not *automatically* vote the right way, because some of them were survivors from previous ministries who held their posts for life and had a measure of independence; but *normally* they would do so, if properly led. There would be an obvious incentive to vote for supply from which salaries and pensions could be paid. In 1669 Danby added to his working list of 92 'such Parliament men as are servants, or have dependence by offices or commands under his Majesty', in addition to other categories, a final one of 'the names of such as have for the most part voted for supplies to his Majesty', for this was the touchstone. After becoming Lord Treasurer in 1673, he was able to add secret service payments, some of which originated as compensation for some loss in connection with the farms of the excise. Browning listed payments of £17,000 known to have been made to 66 members between November 1676 and August 1678 (1951, i. 74, 167–73; iii. 33–42, 50–6; also 1948, pp. 21–36).

The members chosen had rendered loyal service to the king and could be expected to do so again in the future. To the opposition this looked like the crudest form of bribery, and when these activities came to light Henry Nevile in 1680 christened the assembly 'the Pensionary Parliament', a nickname that stuck. There were certainly a few members for whom a seat in the Commons was useful in order to avoid arrest for debt by their creditors or even to sell 'protections' to their supposed servants; and even to those in lesser financial difficulties, the pensions would come as a boon which carried with it political obligations. At the same time, an inspection of the records of the members concerned suggests stongly that many would probably have voted for Danby's Cavalier and Anglican policies anyway, and in that case the significance of the pensions would be mainly as an incentive to appear regularly in the House when votes were taken, rather than attending irregularly or leaving early to go to dinner or to the play. If in many cases the payments took the place of a modern 'whip' in this way, they were none the less useful (and to modern eyes undesirable), particularly when votes were regularly decided by single-figure majorities in the last years of the Cavalier Parliament. Nevertheless, they did not prevent Danby's support from disintegration on the revelation that (on the king's orders) he had been secretly negotiating with Louis

35

XIV, when openly talking of compelling him to end his conquests in Flanders.

We have many fewer names of those members who hobnobbed with foreign ambassadors in a way which would now be thought disgraceful. All foreign envoys believed that the House of Commons was more inclined to the opponents of Louis XIV, whereas (except in 1668) Charles and many of his Court were pro-French, and they also knew that only money from Parliament could enable the king to follow a line of policy and its denial would prevent him from doing so. The hostility of many members to France was genuine, but they tended to give priority to the domestic concerns that weighed more immediately upon them. In 1667, however, it was thought that the Imperial ambassador Lisola was assisting members of the House with information to impeach Clarendon in the interests of rivals who favoured the Habsburgs, and in the next decade or more we know that he and his Confederate colleagues had contacts in the House with whom they discussed the dangers of French domination. They referred to only one or two members by name in their dispatches home, and it has so far been impossible to tell how far the rumours used by French ambassadors to persuade Louis XIV to allocate larger sums for them to use were justified. The States-General voted their ambassador, van Beuningen, a carefully circumscribed sum to spend on dinners for members, and it can easily be imagined that a good deal of wining and dining went on.

Although at one time members could visit the French ambassadors only when muffled in their cloaks, the activities of the French in this connection are more notorious. They included the supply to Coleman, secretary of the Duke of York, of money to distribute among members in order to bring about a dissolution and an end to pressure for a foreign policy directed against France; Coleman's accounts do not survive. Even better known are the payments made to members of the Country Party in 1678–80, when they and the French had quite different resons for wishing to undermine Danby's position. It was very much a marriage of convenience between partners whose attitudes and policies were ultimately entirely opposed. The Country Party needed to know that the French were not at that time subsidizing Charles, and the money would be useful for election purposes. There is no need to suppose that any of the small number of members known by name to have received money changed his basic convictions in the slightest, although the eighteenth-century historian Dalrymple, when he discovered that the Whig martyr Russell had even negotiated with Barrillon, likened it to 'very near the same shock as if I had seen a son turn his back in the day of battle'. The references to Shaftesbury in Barrillon's dispatches do not suggest that he was in close touch with the Frenchman or received money from him; Ralph Montagu's contacts with the ambassador were much closer, but French money only supplemented other motives for his opportunism.

Even the use of methods like this, and the increasing heat of debate, did not mean that the members of the Commons could all be labelled as belonging to a 'Court' or 'Country' party. From time to time Danby and Shaftesbury tried to draw up working lists of their supporters, and the calculation was different each time; nor can the differences be written off as marginal. When he was in the Tower in 1677, Shaftesbury drew up a list of all the members in the House, and alongside the name of each member he put either the letter V for vile (that is, his opponents) or W for worthy; as an extra refinement, he would double or treble the letter – to VVV or WWW – to indicate gradations of either reliability or perhaps regularity of attendance. But although Shaftesbury was as well informed as anyone about politics in this period, there are evidently some cases in which he found reason to change his mind about people, and some cases in which he was proved to be wrong in his assessment. The Cavalier Parliament remained to its end in January 1679 an amorphous body rather than one of clear-cut divisions; Danby was in the end deserted by many members who had previously supported him. There was on each side a core of members who could be depended upon always to vote in accordance with the 'party-line', but there were others who vacillated or chose not to vote. According to Shaftesbury's 1677 estimate, 176 members could be labelled VVV or WWW and could be regarded as committed to one side or the other; 186 were labelled as VV or WW and could be regarded as moderately reliable; and 147 could be labelled with only a single letter (Haley, 1970, pp. 86–105).

Naturally, however, the Exclusion crisis made the party split much deeper. On the question whether James should succeed or not, it was difficult to escape the responsibility of making up one's mind, and afterwards it was even more difficult (though not impossible) to change it. When the three Exclusion Bills discussed in the House were followed by the eviction of Exclusionists from their places as justices of the peace, from the deputy lieutenancies, and from the municipal corporations in the last five years of the reign, it was no coincidence that the classic names of Whig and Tory came into existence, and that 'the rage of party' came to dominate politics both within and outside Parliament.

3 Politics and the People

In Whig history the term 'the people' was ambiguously used, but in this section an attempt will be made to discuss the extent to which all those outside the elite at Whitehall and Westminster were able to participate in the political struggles of the reign. In the words previously quoted from Clarendon's speech in 1661, did others merely consent to be represented by 'the greatest and learnedest . . . and wisest persons' in Parliament?

The fact that the electorate consisted of approximately 300,000 people, or 20–25 per cent of the adult male population, may be regarded in more than one way in comparison with other periods. They constituted a minority of the population, but by no means a negligible minority. The decrease in the value of money and the resulting increase in the number of forty-shilling freeholders with the vote in the counties made it an increasing minority in the sixteenth and seventeenth centuries; as Sir John Plumb has pointed out, when disputes arose on the question of where the right to vote belonged in boroughs, there was a tendency for the opposition to press, with some success, for the wider interpretation and the government for the narrower one. It was only in the Hanoverian period that this process stopped and the electorate ceased to grow appreciably, just when the population began its great spurt. In proportion, the electorate in the reign of Charles II was larger than it was when a demand for parliamentary reform emerged at the end of the eighteenth century, and potentially the voters could bring some influence to bear.

On the other hand, they did not always vote for good political reasons. It is noteworthy that some who were invited to stand for election declined, because they could not afford the election expenses, while in the repeated elections of 1679–81 there were some constituencies which made a virtue of the fact that they were so satisfied with their previous representatives that they made no further calls upon their purse when choosing them once more. Obviously these election expenses were not the cost of printing election leaflets or hiring school halls, but of entertaining the voters. Clarendon read the MPs of 1661 a homily on the vice of 'Excess of Drinking' at elections, and in 1679 a Bill introduced by the opposition for regulating election abuses would, if it had been passed, have provided for declaring ineligible any candidates convicted of treating or bribery (*Parliamentary History*, 1806–20, iv. 206; Jones, 1961, pp. 53–4).

There were, however, important restraints on the electorate. There was not necessarily a contest which proceeded to a poll, and when there was, the candidates were commonly chosen by the country gentry or by a small number of influential people in the boroughs, although even in modern times the number concerned in selecting a candidate is minute in proportion to the electorate. Again, Rousseau later commented that the English people were only free at election times, and as long as the Cavalier Parliament lasted (1661–79) there was no general election at all. This was a subject on which ministers sometimes held different opinions, but the king prudently took the view that a dissolution and the summons of a new Parliament was likely to result in a more troublesome one than that elected in the Cavalier euphoria of 1661. There were by-elections, it is true, in which more than half the members were gradually replaced over the eighteen-year period of the Parliament's existence. In the early years these by-elections created little excitement and the government was even able to find seats for protégés. Sir William Temple optimistically expressed an interest in 'the accomplishment of what his Majesty was once pleased to intend, which was, my election into the Commons House in England, at least whenever there fall any [vacant] in the Cinque Ports, or such a part where a sheet of paper does the business', but his hopes were not gratified and may have been too much influenced by his experience of the Irish House of Commons (Courtenay, 1836, i. 240–1). From 1667, more members with a parliamentarian background began to secure election; in the 1670s, contests in which some excitement was generated and, for instance, Dissenters were recorded as supporting a candidate opposed to Danby attracted attention in some localities. But, as will be seen, it was only when the opportunity of three general elections in 1679–81 was offered that participation could be widespread.

In the meantime, however, other opportunities existed for public opinion, especially in London, to influence members. They not only had to come to Westminster for their sessions, but met next door to Westminster Hall, which was divided up into law-courts, with stalls selling refreshments to those with business there and those who, like Pepys, went there in search of gossip. The resolutions adopted by the two Houses were not officially printed at first, although the No-Popery votes of 1673 appeared in an anonymous pamphlet, and it is striking that when the Commons did decide to print each day's votes in 1680, conservative members regarded this as a dangerous 'appeal to the people'. Although a few members such as Anchitel Grey kept notes of debates for their own use there, these were supposed to be strictly confidential; ironically, the first pamphlet publication, *A Letter from a Person of Quality to his Friend in the Country* (perhaps written by John Locke at Shaftesbury's dictation), described the arguments in the Lords over Danby's non-resistance test of 1675, and the House ordered it to be burnt by the common hangman at the Royal Exchange and also in Old Palace Yard at Westminster. It was of some significance that at first the details of Oates's Popish Plot stories to the Commons were not officially revealed to the public. Yet obviously it was quite impossible to maintain the confidentiality of parliamentary proceedings, and enough leaked out for a public opinion to form which was bound to react upon members.

This public opinion was particularly important in the City. On the Exchange merchants would inevitably discuss the political background to the government's latest request for loans and were concerned about the course of foreign policy and whether the Commons would vote money to support it. In 1664 it was the conjunction of opinion in the City with the Court and Commons which led to overwhelming pressure for war with the Dutch; in general, merchant opinion believed that the balance of trade with France was unfavourable and that with Spain was favourable, and, for instance, in 1673 the fear that the French alliance would lead England into war with Spain was one factor in leading opinion in the City and in the Commons to press for abandoning the third Dutch war. Whether the number of Dissenters in the City influenced the decline of pressure in the Commons for the persecution of Puritans and the growth of pressure for measures against Popery is more difficult to estimate, but it must surely have been a factor in the consciousness of members and of ministers. In 1676, one Francis Jenks, a linen draper in Cornhill, got up in the annual meeting for the election of sheriffs at the Guildhall and made a sensational speech attacking the danger to trade from France and to the Protestant religion, and asking for a Common Council to be called to petition the king for a new Parliament. His call was evaded, but this was the beginning of a definite attempt over the next six years to involve the institutions of the City in the national political disputes; Shaftesbury and Buckingham both took houses in the City and became members of livery companies.

Members and citizens talked politics in the coffee-houses, where satirical poems with titles like 'Last Instructions to a Painter' and anonymous pamphlets were passed from hand to hand and discussed over the newly fashionable drinks of

42

coffee, chocolate, tea and sherbet. Inevitably there was a tendency for these writings to become critical and even scandalous (from the government's point of view); some coffee-houses were a nucleus for the eventual development of political clubs. On at least two occasions, the government contemplated closing them down because coffee and talk were so dangerous, but shrank from the unpopularity (and perhaps the loss of revenue) that would have resulted.

For their use, a pamphlet literature of discontent came into existence. Nominally it should have been prevented by the provisions of the Licensing Act of 1662, which set up a censorship of all printed works, in which 'all books of history' as well as 'other books concerning any affairs of state' had to be licensed by one of the secretaries of state, whose messengers were to have powers of search for unauthorized books. These official restrictions undoubtedly acted as a deterrent upon works with the author's name upon them, added a spice of danger and correspondingly augmented the value of material which escaped the censor, but they could not hope to be completely effective. The printing presses of the time were not elaborate and were even portable; they could be concealed easily enough in the backstreets of 'the best lurking place of Europe', and hawkers were not lacking to take the risk of selling libels. In December 1667, Clarendon wrote an apologia to the House of Lords for fleeing the country instead of remaining to stand trial. The House ordered it to be solemnly burnt by the hangman, but it was not long before copies of the letter were on sale openly for two pence a sheet at the very place where it had been officially burnt (MS Carte 36, fo. 41). We have little knowledge of pamphlet circulation, but we know of a reference to a printer who produced '4 or 6,000 copies' of *England's Appeal from the Private Cabal at Whitehall* (1673), as though this was only one of several impressions, and each copy would be read by or to more than one person. The *Appeal* was the most important of several pieces of Dutch propaganda which Charles and his ministers believed

43

to have turned public opinion against the Dutch war, and which were distributed without the government being able to seize those responsible (Haley, 1953, p. 100).

It is less easy to determine how much news reached the provinces. The newsletters to which some gentry subscribed were undoubtedly rather bald, but they do indicate an interest in what was going on, and pamphlets like the *Appeal* were distributed in provincial centres as well as in London. But the easiest and least traceable means of communication was by word of mouth. At the lowest level, members had to defend their votes of taxation, at a time when rumours of waste were widespread, to their fellow-taxpayers; but in addition there was constant traffic to and from London for reasons of business, trade, litigation or fashion, while co-religionaries kept in touch with one another for reasons of their own. The nationwide excitement of the Popish Plot and Exclusion crisis is explicable only on the basis that knowledge of what was going on, or supposed to be going on, was widespread.

The first result of the dissolution of the Cavalier Parliament in January 1679 was the lapsing of the Licensing Act of 1662. Attempts were made to justify continued restriction of the Press under the common law instead of statute, but in practice these collapsed in the next few years, and a flood of pamphlets and newspapers appeared. They varied from the crudest exaggeration of the dangers of Popery to a much more rational examination of the issues, which has to some extent been obscured by historians' natural revulsion in more modern times at the excesses of many pamphleteers. They were dominated by the opposition at least until the government reacted through the more skilled journalism of L'Estrange's *Observator* and Flatman's *Heraclitus Ridens*, which appeared from the spring of 1681 in regular issues at intervals of a few days to reveal the weaknesses in the case put forward by the pro-Oates journals. Some of the pamphlets were no doubt prompted by Whig politicians, including those with a serious political case to argue, whereas others appeared for more commercial reasons to appeal to an obvious market for 'No-Popery' literature, but the volume of material that existed is the clearest indication that there was an extensive and literate public interested in it.

According to Plumb, 'by the end of the Exclusion Crisis more men had become involved in parliamentary politics in the constituencies than ever before in the history of Parliament' (1967, p. 4–7). In 1679, the competition for vacancies, the number of contested elections and the intensity of partisan feeling greatly increased, and it was the opposition which profited. If there were fewer contests in the later Exclusion Parliaments, it was because the Tories did not find it worth while to challenge the re-election of Whig members in the former Parliament. From the accounts of elections which we possess (and it is significant that they are more numerous than ever before), we can see what pains were taken to mobilize support, with large numbers of followers accompanying their leaders to the poll in the more open constituencies. On many occasions, the presence of Dissenters among the supporters of Whigs was commented upon, and even though experience of the Civil War and Commonwealth had greatly reduced the appeal of Puritanism to the country gentry, it is remarkable that sixty or seventy of the members of the Exclusion Parliaments were Dissenters or probable Dissenters, and about the same proportion consisted of ex-Puritans who had conformed to the established church after the Restoration, but might be suspected of favouring some indulgence to Protestant non-conformists. There was, however, little change in the social composition of those elected; the proportion of country gentry even increased slightly, and if the number of merchants in the House also increased (if only to about 10 per cent), it was at the expense of a halving of the number of government officials. The pattern of distribution of income also remained much the same, according to the tables of the *History of Parliament* (Henning, 1983), with the proportion of 'rich' or 'very rich' members (that is, with an income over £1,000 per annum) remaining roughly constant. What had changed was the dependence of members upon the electorate.

Moreover, it became a definite feature of Whig policy to involve popular support, in the provinces as well as in London, at times other than elections. The Duke of Monmouth showed himself to the populace on three progresses – to the West Country in 1680, Chichester in 1681 and Cheshire in 1682 – like a modern political leader. When he visited Exeter, the crowd was estimated at 10,000 on horseback and 1,500 on foot; even if this was an exaggeration, there can be no doubt of the warmth of his welcome in places which the king did not visit. When the Parliament that was elected in the autumn of 1679 was promptly prorogued by Charles before it was allowed to meet, Shaftesbury organized the presentation of petitions that it be permitted to sit. The model for these was supplied from London, with even printed forms for subscription; some petitions were sent on behalf of the local grand jury, but in other cases attempts were made to collect the largest possible number of signatures. In London itself, tables, pens, ink and forms were placed in taverns and at the Royal Exchange. Proclamations forbidding the petitions were ignored and, in all, the signatures were counted in tens of thousands. The petition in the name of Westminster and Southwark was said to contain 50,000 or 60,000 signatures, and 'Tom of Ten Thousand' presented a petition with 30,000 names from Wiltshire. The success of the technique was shown by the organization of counter-addresses ab-horring the petitions, although the number of people who signed was not by any means as great.

According to their opponents, Monmouth's progresses were attended only by 'the common people' or even 'the rabble', while respectable people stayed away, and the usual criticisms were made of the mass petitions, although with what accuracy it is impossible to say. It was alleged that many signatures were forged or the result of bribery, and others looked like 'insects crawling about' or 'the hieroglyphics of clowns'; it was pointed out 'how absurd it was for workmen, before even washing their hands, to plunge into these secrets of government, and give the King instructions as to when it was politic to hold a Parliament – as if they knew more about affairs of state than the King or his Council!' An attempt was made to frighten Anglicans by stating that 'in all the length from Temple Bar to Whitehall' there were not twenty signatories 'on both sides of the way to the street (and those are known to be the best men) . . . excepting only such as are constant conventiclers' (North, 1740, pp. 542–4; Haley, 1968, p. 562).

This picture of class conflict between 'the common people' and 'the gentlemen', and between Anglicans and Dissenters should not be accepted at its full face value. Certainly, there was a strand of Whig propaganda which attacked 'Tantivy' country squires who were supposedly subservient to their parsons, but it was also part of government propaganda to scare off the well-to-do and the Churchmen (who outnumbered the Dissenters) by exaggerating the prospects of social and religious disorder. Country gentlemen did meet Monmouth; as we have seen, the Exclusionist majorities in the House of Commons were elected on a limited franchise, and consisted mainly of country gentry and Anglicans, and the very fact that it was necessary to purge the commissions of the peace extensively in 1680 shows the measure of support for Exclusion among prominent members of county society. Charles criticized 'Tom of Ten Thousand', the wealthy owner of Longleat, for presenting the Wiltshire petition, saying 'that he did not think a gentleman of his fortune and estate would have concerned himself in anything that looked like a rebellion', but Whigs generally were not poor or obscure men. The jury which acquitted Shaftesbury in 1681 was estimated to be worth a million pounds in all. It was an essential feature of the 'No-Popery' slogan that it appealed alike to the owner of Longleat, to wealthy City magnates, to artisans like Stephen College, 'the Protestant joiner', and to convinced Protestants – Anglicans as well as Dissenters. Otherwise they would not have dominated the House of

Commons to the point where the Tories never ventured even to a vote against the second and third Exclusion Bills.

Nevertheless it does also seem to be true that the Whigs were much readier than the Tories to appeal for support from those outside what would have been the 'political nation' in more normal times, and from Puritans who had been excluded from national politics since the Commonwealth and persecuted at intervals since then. In contrast to Tory propaganda that the Exclusionists were the party of 'the rabble', Whig propaganda claimed that they represented the whole nation, and it is significant that from the summer of 1681 the government, in its turn, took every opportunity to encourage Tory addresses, whether thanking the king for his *Declaration* explaining the dissolution of the Oxford Parliament or, two years later, congratulating him on the failure of the Rye House conspirators. If nothing else, they conceded the principle that politics was a matter of widespread public concern.

Into this pattern we must fit the famous instructions which many Whig constituents provided for members elected to the Oxford Parliament of 1681, and in which some historians have even seen the origins of the modern democratic 'mandate' from electorates to their representatives. These instructions to members were not identical, but the similarities are sufficient to suggest strongly that they were encouraged by a central source, presumably Shaftesbury. They laid it down that their members were not to grant money until provision had been made to exclude a Popish successor, and moreover, that no 'expedient' less than exclusion should be accepted. Many addresses also included demands for annual, or at least frequent, Parliaments to escape from the king's powers of prorogation and dissolution as it suited him. (Browning, 1953, pp. 256–7).

It has often been suggestd that these instructions and much else was planned from a central source in the Green Ribbon Club, in the King's Head tavern at the corner of Chancery Lane, but the available evidence does not permit

48

us to state conclusively that these were much more than social gatherings of leading Whigs who financed the famous Pope-burning processions of these years. In Pepys's list of the members of the Green Ribbon Club, Shaftesbury and Buckingham were not included, and it is not easy to see why a confidential meeting to discuss party tactics should have been held at the King's Head tavern, rather than privately in Shaftesbury's own house. The Green Ribbon Club – and we cannot say whether the name, with its Leveller connotations, was adopted by its members or attached to it in derision by its enemies – was in any case only one of several Whig clubs, just as there were also Tory clubs, forerunners of the later party clubs of the eighteenth century, which lubricated social contacts among party members rather than formally planning political tactics (Allen, 1979, p. 557).

The question remains whether the Whig appeal for 'out-of-doors' support extended to more unorthodox and even violent forms of action. The use of the word 'mob' by Tories like Roger North, and descriptions of the enormous Pope-burning processions on Guy Fawkes Day or on the anniversary of Queen Elizabeth's accession, another Protestant occasion, have perhaps led to exaggerated views of the exercise of intimidation upon fellow-Londoners. They were the equivalent of the modern demonstration by which the party faithful build up their psychological confidence by the knowledge of their own strength – and then return peaceably home. There was rowdyism, but nothing like a revolutionary *journée*. There were bonfires to celebrate political events more directly; thus when Monmouth returned secretly from exile in November 1679, within an hour (though it was still dark) church bells were ringing, by eight o'clock copies of verses in his honour were being sold in the streets (surely the result of some organization) and that evening there were more than sixty bonfires between Temple Bar and Charing Cross alone. The 'rabble' stopped the Lord Chancellor's coach and made him drink Monmouth's health, while others were told to drink it in kennel water or to pay for better liquor. On the other hand, when James returned from Scotland in April 1682, there were few bonfires in the City, but many in the neighbourhood of Whitehall and St James's, and it was Shaftesbury's turn to be burnt instead of Guy Fawkes.

Shaftesbury's acquittal by the ignoramus jury at the end of 1681 was accompanied and followed by scenes of rowdiness on the part of 'a rattle-headed scum of the *Canaglia*', which were later used as the basis for an attack on the City of London's charter, on the ground that the corporation had failed to keep order. But there seems to have been no bloodshed, and above all there was no attempt to turn the excitement and rowdiness into an armed coup. There may be some truth in the view that the government was able to rely on the support of the trained bands to prevent the situation getting out of hand in the City, but even supposing that none of the rank and file sympathized with the Whigs, it is doubtful whether they could have kept control over a planned attempt at riot. Not only parliamentary elections, but also the annual elections of sheriffs caused problems for the authorities, whose means of keeping order (supposing that they wished to do so) were slender. But the significant thing is that, whatever the demonstrations within the City from time to time, they were never converted into direct action at Whitehall and Westminster. There was no equivalent to the mobs which had swarmed outside Charles I's palace at the time of Strafford's attainder in 1641, and the rejection of the Exclusion Bill by the House of Lords in 1680 was not followed by a repetition of the intimidation that had led the bishops and others to absent themselves from debates of the Upper House in the winter of 1641/2.

The significance of Shaftesbury's supposed 'brisk boys' at Wapping is that, whether armed with a 'Protestant flail' or not, the sailors of that suburb never actually emerged to challenge the government. There was never the slightest prospect that Charles II would have to leave his capital as his father had done, and he continued to dine in the City from time to time, even taking his brother with him on occasion. Although he had the advantage of a larger force of guards than his father to act as a deterrent, the standing army in England amounted to no more than 6,000 after the forces raised temporarily for the needs of Charles II's foreign policy in 1678 had been disbanded; how useful the part-time forces of the militia would have been is questionable. In the last resort, the absence of anything like a *journée* (or worse) must be attributed to the marked preferences of most Whig leaders for constitutional methods, and a sensitiveness to the Tory propaganda argument that ' '41 is come again' and would be followed by another civil war if care was not taken. Whatever they might feel about the danger of a Popish successor, they had always professed loyalty to Charles II and had no wish to go back to a Commonwealth. When the 1681 Parliament was dissolved and early hopes of a constitutional solution to the problem of the succession ended, Shaftesbury, an 'old man in a hurry', probably contemplated rebellion and the confessions of the later Rye House conspirators implicated others. The essential fact remains, however, that in the concluding years of the reign no rebellion actually broke out, even when, without a Parliament, a party amounting to half the country was left with no constitutional platform from which to put forward its claims.

At the centre of much of this activity were the apprehensions raised by the king's brother, and it is time now to analyse why this was so, and to place the problem of the succession in the context of the political difficulties earlier in the reign.

4 Politics and Dynastic Accidents

On Easter Sunday, 1673, it was noticed that for the second year in succession James, Duke of York, abstained from taking communion with his brother according to the rites of the Church of England. In another two months, he failed to fulfil the requirements of the new Test Act and make the anti-Catholic declaration which would have qualified him to retain his position as Lord High Admiral. Although he continued to accompany Charles to ordinary services at the royal chapel until 1676, it was now an open secret that James was a Catholic.

For the next generation this was the central fact in English politics. The religion of the king's brother would have been important in any event, but it was made infinitely more so by the dynastic accident that though Charles had numerous illegitimate children (he recognized fourteen), he had no legitimate ones. It was even supposed that Clarendon had arranged deliberately to marry Charles to a barren queen so that the throne might pass to his son-in-law James (who had married Anne Hyde) and thus to his own grandchildren, although there are no grounds for the historian to believe that this suspicion was true. In 1673, therefore, it became clear that the throne of England could be expected to pass to a Popish successor, and this realization combined with other events in that year to create doubts about the Protestant soundness of the government's whole policy, both domestic and foreign, and so transformed people's political attitudes.

This does not mean that previously relations between Charles and Parliament had run smoothly, but only that until the middle of the reign they had not been bedevilled by doubts about the government's fundamental policy objectives. Previously there had been Cavalier criticisms that the government was too soft on former Puritan enemies, and that large grants of taxation had resulted only in waste, extravagance, embezzlement and the miscarriages of the Dutch war of 1664–7. With a few exceptions, however, criticisms in the 1660s were criticisms of tactics and maladministration, embarrassing enough to the reputation of those in government and obstructing further grants of money, but not really basic.

The Convention of 1660 had been elected before the king's return, and nominally Cavaliers or the sons of Cavaliers had been declared ineligible for election, although this provision had not always been adhered to. The result had been that the Convention had contained a large number of ex-Parliamentarians and even ex-supporters of the Commonwealth, and the government's preoccupations had been to arrange for the disbandment of the Cromwellian Army, to lay the basis for an adequate peacetime revenue, and to obstruct the desire of Puritan MPs to enact a religious settlement which suited them. By the end of 1660 it appeared that these aims had been fairly satisfactorily accomplished. The Army was paid off or shipped off to Portugal. The sum of £1.2 million per annum had been fixed for the king's ordinary peacetime revenue. The report from the Commons committee naming this not unreasonable figure (in terms of the revenue of Charles I) had been made by the Solicitor-General, and presumably represented a government view; it was not yet clear that the taxes actually voted would not yield this amount. A statute to settle religious problems had been successfully avoided so that they could be left to a later Parliament of Cavaliers. It is not surprising that in his speech at the dissolution

Charles declared that 'when God brought me hither, I brought with me an extraordinary affection and esteem for parliament', and went on to propose for the Convention the nickname of 'The Healing and Blessed Parliament', although it was stretching his intentions rather a lot to say 'I shall not more propose any one real good to myself in my actions than this, What is a parliament like to think of this action or this counsel?' (*Parliamentary History*, 1806–20, iv. 170).

If he adhered to this in later life it was not quite in the spirit that he implied in this speech to the Convention; but when in the following spring a new Parliament assembled consisting predominantly of Cavaliers, he congratulated himself 'that there are not many of you who are not particularly known to me' and looked forward to concurring with them 'in all things which may advance the peace, plenty and prosperity of the nation' (p. 179). The difficulty was that they were excessively Royalist at a time when Charles and Clarendon did not yet feel absolutely secure from a new Puritan rebellion. They had to be restrained from overthrowing the Convention's Act of Indemnity to their former enemies, and the Commons in effect insisted that the Act of Uniformity should be more extreme than Charles and Clarendon originally contemplated. There has been much difference of opinion over Clarendon's attitude at this point: writers at one extreme recall Clarendon's opposition to concessions to Presbyterians to secure the king's restoration and rely on Clarendon's own autobiographical and pro-Anglican account, whereas at the opposite extreme the inconsistencies and distortions in that record are pointed out and it has even been argued that he was a supporter of toleration. For the present writer the key seems to lie in the Chancellor's opening speech to the Cavalier Parliament, in which he described them as 'the great physicians of the kingdom' with delicate and wayward patients 'to whom they ought not to prescribe remedies, how well compounded soever, too nauseous to their stomachs and appetites, or to their fancy'; they should 'make a temporary provision of an easier and a lighter yoke, till by living in a wholesome air, by the benefit of a soberer conversation, by keeping a better diet . . .' they return to health; but at the same time they must see that 'under pretence of liberty of conscience, men may not be absolved from all the obligations of law and conscience' (*Parliamentary History*, 1806–20, iv. 186). This seems to have meant in practice that there should be an established episcopal church, in essentials the same as the pre-war Church of England, as a prop to royal authority, but with sufficient concessions in non-essentials to comprehend as many former Puritans as possible, incidentally doing something to meet the promise of 'liberty to tender consciences' in the Declaration of Breda, and so to avoid driving opponents into rebellion.

If this was Clarendon's policy as a statesman (whatever his own personal preferences in an ideal world), it was foiled by the Commons' insistence on a Prayer Book with only minor alterations from the book of 1559 and an Act of Uniformity which ejected a substantial minority of Puritan ministers. Clarendon's own mitigating amendments in the Lords were rejected and new clauses put forward in the lower House to make the Act more rigorous. Moreover in 1663 they rapidly made it clear that they would not adopt a Declaration of Indulgence which Charles had issued in the previous December, and now Clarendon himself spoke vehemently against a Bill in the Lords which would have made it possible for the king to grant dispensations to ministers. In 1664, the Commons insisted on a Conventicle Act, which for the first time imposed penalties on lay dissenters as well, and although it was rather spasmodically and erratically enforced, they insisted on a strengthened Conventicle Act as 'the price of money' in 1670.

In all this they were more Royalist and more Anglican than the king, who privately wanted some indulgence for his Catholic friends. They did not think of themselves as acting in a spirit of opposition, however, and were able to reconcile their actions the more easily because they knew that among the king's own privy councillors there were differences of opinion, which encouraged them to press their own point of view. In the years that followed, this developed further with the rivalries between Clarendon and his critics within the council extending, during parliamentary sessions, to the House of Commons.

In 1664 Charles, Clarendon and Lord Treasurer Southampton were reluctantly swept into war with the Dutch under the combined pressure of courtiers, City and Commons, before proper preparations had been made and before order had been brought into the king's finances. The unprecedentedly large taxes voted for the purpose and the euphoria generated by the opening victory off Lowestoft only made the contrast worse when the navy failed to make any decisive impact upon the Dutch, and evident mismanagement was accompanied by the blows to morale – as well as to income – dealt by the Plague and Fire, until the culmination was reached of the humiliating Dutch invasion of the Medway, and Clarendon was removed as the scapegoat.

In the years 1666–8 the Commons, when they were allowed to meet, were encouraged by Clarendon's enemies among the ministers to develop from a house of courtiers into a house of critics. Instinctively, rather than in order to reach any long-term constitutional objective, they found themselves calling for a parliamentary commission of inquiry into the way the king's ministers had spent their taxes. They agitated against the king's and Clarendon's wishes for a ban on the import of Irish cattle and inserted the word 'nuisance' to prevent the king from dispensing anyone from the Bill's provisions. They not only impeached Clarendon (with encouragement from the king as well as other ministers), but inserted into the Act for his banishment a clause preventing the king from pardoning him without Parliament's consent. And they sought to hold others responsible for the various 'miscarriages' of the war.

All this would have been unthinkable to members when they first assembled in 1661. Just as the king began without

56

any systematic desire to 'make himself absolute', so did they begin without any plan to 'restrict the royal prerogative', and we should guard against any tendency to think of them as unanimous at any time. None the less, just as Charles tended, as time went on, to use every opportunity to gain greater freedom for himself, the majority of the Commons felt free to press their own grievances. It must be remembered that behind all else lay Charles's desperate need for money and his growing reluctance to call a troublesome and unmanageable Parliament unless he could expect them to provide it.

However, in some respects matters improved a little as the second period of the reign, that of the so-called Cabal, proceeded. The Triple Alliance of 1668 gained the government some much-needed popularity, and there is some significance in the fact that later in the same year Louis XIV felt it safe to offer to guarantee Charles help against rebels, something that he had evaded previously. In the sessions of 1670 and 1671 the Commons were rather more generous than before, although they did not grant all that the king needed, as memories of the war receded a little.

Ironically, the grant in the last session was obtained in response to Lord Keeper Bridgeman's appeal for money to support the Triple Alliance. No Parliament was called between April 1671 and February 1673, and in the meantime Charles, using principally the money liberated by the Stop of the Exchequer, reversed his foreign policy and again declared war against the Dutch, and by virtue of the royal prerogative rather than a parliamentary repeal of the penal laws, issued the Declaration of Indulgence to lift penalties from Catholic recusants as well as Dissenters. Two months later Louis XIV also declared war against the Dutch, and although he therefore appeared at first sight to be an ally in an English quarrel and his help could not be neglected, England was now co-operating, in an alliance whose terms were not public, with the leading authoritarian and Catholic monarch in Europe.

When Parliament had to be summoned again in February

ie. Louis XIV (well done!)

1673 to grant the money without which a second campaign could not be contemplated, the Commons did not refuse it, but by a substantial majority, in which country Cavaliers played a prominent part, insisted on the revocation of the Declaration of Indulgence and the passing of a Test Act to exclude Catholics from all civil and military office. It became known that in the House of Lords Charles II's Lord Treasurer, Clifford, a strong supporter of the Duke of York, made a vehement but vain attack on this Test Act just ten days before the Easter Sunday on which James refused communion. When James did not continue as Lord High Admiral (although he had commanded the fleet at Sole Bay in the previous year) and Clifford also withdrew after an incident in which his coach overturned in the Strand and spilled out, along with the Treasurer, a priest in full robes on the way to mass, fears of Popery in high quarters were augmented. In the next few months Dutch propaganda played on the widespread suspicion that the French alliance contained secret clauses in addition to those providing for war against the Dutch. In view of this suspicion, it was fortunate that no one knew of the Treaty of Dover and its precise contents, in which Charles undertook to declare himself a Catholic and Louis promised both money and men to assist him.

II

It was in this context that people became aware that the heir to the throne was a Catholic, but it is also noteworthy that there are signs of his unpopularity in some quarters well before his religion was known.

In February 1661, Pepys recorded his dislike of the possibility that James might come to the throne, 'he being a professed friend to the Catholics', but he nowhere else refers to rumours relating to James's religion. In October 1662, however, he first reported rumours that the Duke of Monmouth was really Charles's legitimate son, and early in the following year commented that James's popularity was

58

'not great'. After the courage which James showed in the naval victory off Lowestoft in 1665, he gained greatly in the general esteem, received concrete evidence of this in the shape of a generous financial reward from Parliament and ever afterwards retained a rather pathetic memory of being 'the darling of the nation' at this time. By 1667, however, his authoritarian temperament was already disliked; when there was distrust that the troops raised to resist a possible Dutch invasion would be used to enforce government policy, he was credited with advising the king to raise money by royal prerogative, with wanting to have a standing army and with favouring a 'government like that of France'.

The fact that he was Clarendon's son-in-law and tried to prevent his dismissal did not help and led to a spate of rumours that he was at odds with the king and that Monmouth would be declared legitimate. In 1670, there was widespread gossip that the private Bill for the divorce of Lord Roos was intended by Buckingham, Shaftesbury and others to provide a precedent for the king to divorce Queen Catherine for barrenness. This was the time when Charles began to make it a practice to attend debates in the Lords. In reality, all the fuss simply provided Charles with an excellent means of diverting attention from the final negotiations leading to the Treaty of Dover, but it is a clear indication that there were already those who favoured action to exclude James from the succession.

For courtiers, considerations of self-interest were involved as well as dislike of James's temperament and attitudes. To set oneself against the obvious heir to the throne, who might one day be the fountain of the royal patronage described earlier, was a bold step to take. The best illustration is to be found in a later episode in 1679. James had been sent into exile at the prompting of Charles's ministers in an attempt to avert attack by Parliament, which was soon to meet, but when the king fell seriously ill he was promptly recalled to the royal bedside. Courtiers flocked to pay their respects to the man who might soon be on the throne. 'Who goes for Windsor?' was the cynical cry in London, and there was 'more kneeling within these walls, than in four months before'. Even Monmouth's cronies found it prudent to go, but when Sir Thomas Armstrong approached him James ostentatiously turned his back on him. A man who offended James's hard and unforgiving nature risked his personal prospects (Haley, 1968, p. 546).

It is the more significant that by 1670 there were already people who were prepared to take this risk. It is true that James's private conversion by the Jesuit Father Simons may have taken place in 1669, but it could not have been positively known at that time.

If James had not been a Catholic or had been prepared, like his brother, to conceal a preference for Catholicism, his natural right to succeed would probably have been accepted by all, should Charles not remarry. If a Catholic ruler had not been James, but someone more subtle, flexible and accommodating, it is just possible that his right might have been accepted with equal agreement. It was the combination of James and Catholicism that seemed disastrous.

In our ecumenical age, the 'No-Popery' agitation with its wild exaggerations seems repellent. Nevertheless the fears of Popery were genuine and not just a cover for political ambition. Blaming Catholics for the Great Fire of London was no more sensible than blaming the French or the Dutch, but at the time of the fire in 1666 it led to no serious political action, and it is even possible that under a monarch and with an heir of unimpeachable Protestant soundness Catholics would more and more have been left alone, though not with equal rights, as in the United Provinces. The succession question, however, changed the whole complexion of affairs; one member, Henry Powle, opposed the Declaration of Indulgence because 'the King by this may change religion as he pleases; we are confident of him [Charles], but knows not what succession may be' (Grey, iii. 16).

60

Those with a knowledge of the history of the English Reformation were well aware that with the aid of the immense power and patronage at his or her disposal, every monarch had carried through his or her different religious settlement. But also every observer of the contemporary scene knew that effectively the principle of *cuius regio eius religio* operated. No Catholic king ruled over a Protestant people. In France there was a Huguenot minority tolerated by virtue of the Edict of Nantes, but the concessions made by Henry IV were withdrawn by his grandson on the patently insincere ground that they were no longer necessary; and it is a fallacy to suppose that Englishmen were not aware that Louis XIV was whittling down the freedoms of the Huguenots well before the Revocation of the Edict in 1685. There were French Protestants in London, and in 1669 the French ambassador reported concern about the measures that Louis was taking against the Huguenots of Poitou.

Recent estimates of the number of Catholics in England at that time have varied from a mere 1.6 to 4 per cent, and it is easy to say that the fears of widespread conversions under royal influence (like the sensational conversion of Turenne in France) were exaggerated, and that the Whigs' attacks on opponents as 'popishly affected' were an obvious smear. But to Londoners, it was also obvious that the concentration of Catholics in the 'corridors of power' at Whitehall, St James's and Somerset House was much greater than 1.6 per cent, greater indeed than at the Court of Charles I. Few except Titus Oates supposed that Queen Catherine of Braganza was as dangerous as Henrietta Maria had once been considered to be; but there were many who lived under her protection, and numerous sightseers who, like Pepys, observed mass at Somerset House. The household of the Duke and Duchess of York contained people like Richard Talbot, who was singled out by name by the House of Commons in 1673 for a recommendation that he should be immediately dismissed from all commands, military and civil, and forbidden all access to Charles II's Court. He was to gain notoriety in the next reign as Earl of Tyrconnel; Edward Coleman's indiscreet hopes of the good times coming for Catholics when James succeeded, and his correspondence with Louis XIV's confessor, brought ruin to himself and danger to his co-religionaries in the Popish Plot in 1678. It was known that Lady Castlemaine and the Duchess of Portsmouth were Catholics, and that the French ambassador frequented Court and appeared to be on confidential terms with both Charles and James, and no one could fail to observe the number of Catholic hangers-on. It was easy to jump to the obvious conclusion that Catholic influence was dangerously great.

Fears of Popery were wildly exaggerated and Catholics generally had no revolutionary aims, but the suspicions were genuine and cannot be written off as 'hysteria' or the creation of interested politicians. The House of Commons had drawn up addresses against the growth of Popery, for instance in 1671, referring particularly to the numbers of Catholics frequenting Whitehall and Westminster. There are hints of suspicions of the king's own soundness to the Church of England, but ironically, in repudiating the calumnies against Charles I, the Cavalier Parliament in 1661 had made it treasonable to declare that the king was a Papist. Thus, until Charles declared himself a Catholic on his death-bed, the generally expressed view contrasted his Protestantism with the undoubted Catholicism of his heir, for which in the end innocent Catholics suffered.

III

If the first 'dynastic accident' of the reign was Charles's lack of legitimate children, the second was that, although James had fifteen (as well as some who were illegitimate), there were few who survived even the early weeks of infancy. No legitimate son survived until 1688, when a belief that he had contracted venereal disease and communicated it to his queen was one reason why the Old Pretender was widely believed to be a changeling. Until

62

then he had two daughters by his first marriage, Mary and Anne, but they might at any time be superseded in their rights to the succession if a healthy son was born.

In 1673, James married a second time. His chosen bride was Mary of Modena, a French protégée of 15, the last of whose eight pregnancies was not until 1692. Until 1688 it was a matter of doubt whether a healthy son would be born to be brought up a Catholic and to carry on a Catholic dynasty: if such a boy had been born in the 1670s (and a Duke of Cambridge did live for five weeks in 1677), it would have affected the political situation, but in the absence of one, Mary and Anne were next in line. Whether they were sound Protestants, and whom they would marry when they grew up, remained to be seen.

The House of Commons vainly passed an address to try to prevent the consummation of James's proxy marriage, but thereafter had to accept the situation. Charles would have liked to resolve the situation by persuading James to return officially to the Church of England, and, in spite of his secret promises in the Treaty of Dover, complained bitterly to the French ambassador that his brother's behaviour was the cause of his difficulties. It would obviously have been to James's political advantage to make the pretence of Anglicanism which Charles wanted, but stubbornly and honourably he adhered to his resolve. No death-bed conversion would have been sufficient for him, and in any case few would have believed in such a pretence. The outline of the situation was therefore fixed.

The first reaction of the opponents of James was to revive the plan to divorce Charles and enable him to remarry. This possibility was talked of on several occasions in 1673 and was particularly associated with the name of Shaftesbury. It probably remained Shaftesbury's favourite solution to the problem; it was revived even during the Popish Plot. It would have eliminated the uncertainty about a possible son for James, and the fact is striking that the Whig leader never formally committed himself to the patently very dubious claims of Monmouth. It would have been the solution likely to have commanded widest support, and although James might have regarded it as against canon law, he had never come out in open opposition to his brother or formed the kind of 'reversionary interest' that existed in the Hanoverian period, in response to his father's dying adjurations to him never to be separated from Charles. But it was impossible to divorce a man who did not wish to be divorced, and although Charles was sometimes rumoured to be ready to comply, he remained honourably faithful to the queen in that respect, if not in the familiar sense of the word, even though he could have bought off much of the opposition by consenting. Like Catherine of Aragon, Catherine of Braganza influenced the situation by remaining alive and, unlike her namesake, even survived her husband.

The Commons, by making plain their refusal to vote money for another campaign, were able to oblige Charles to make peace with the United Provinces at the Treaty of Westminster (February 1674), but still had reason to complain of the recruiting which was permitted for the British regiments to the pay of Louis XIV, so that the pro-French inclinations of the royal brothers were still suspected. Over the whole of his career James's attitude to France was not so simply subservient as people supposed, but it was only when he was king and in control that he could afford to make a show of independence to escape from the imputation of being pro-French. In Charles's reign, at least, the supposition that he was not averse to Louis XIV's gains on the Continent was not unjust. He was commonly supposed to exercise his influence on the French side.

If the Commons saw the end of the Dutch war and the disintegration of the Cabal with the departure and death of Clifford, the dismissal of Shaftesbury and the fading of Arlington and Buckingham from the king's counsels, the Country Party were able to make no further progress in the third period of the reign (1673–8). A move for a divorce was futile, and even if Monmouth had been disposed to abandon the court and ally with them, there was no evidence of his mother's marriage lines and no myth of the 'Black Box' as yet. Nor had the Country Party any coherent long-term programme to restrict the royal prerogative, although individuals might from time to time make proposals which would have that effect. In 1674, for the first time, a Habeas Corpus Bill to stop the loopholes in that procedure received three readings; a Test Bill would have eliminated Catholics from Parliament, and another Bill would have laid down that judges held office during good behaviour and no longer at the royal pleasure, one member bluntly declaring that 'though we have no reason to misdoubt the King, yet we tremble to think what we may come under.' The Lords discussed a proposal to prevent a prince of the blood marrying a Catholic in future without the consent of Parliament, and all this was said to be the work of 'a combination betwixt the discontented and turbulent Commons in the south-east corner of our house and some hotspurs in the Upper' (Christie, 1874, ii. 156–7). But all this, and a measured direct attack on James, was obstructed when the king prorogued Parliament, and similar Bills were also lost at the end of the next three sessions.

In the next years Danby recovered some of the lost ground, from the king's point of view, by financial measures aimed at reducing the government's dependence upon Parliament, by a policy of religious orthodoxy which, through enforcing both the Conventicle Acts against Dissenters and the penal laws against Catholics, appealed to the Anglican and Cavalier susceptibilities of members, and by organizing a Court Party, using the methods previously described. In so doing he alienated James, but had some success in redressing the balance in the Commons until Court and Country were approximately equal. He benefited from the fact that in 1677 Shaftesbury made the mistake of arguing that Parliament had been dissolved because there had been an interval of over a year between sessions, an argument never likely to commend itself to members of the Commons, who would have to stand for re-election, and condemned by the Lords, who committed Shaftesbury to the Tower for contempt.

Danby also hoped to deal with the imputation that Charles II's government was pro-French by a foreign policy aimed at bringing the continental war to an end and restricting Louis XIV's conquests in Flanders. He knew nothing of the way in which Charles had put himself into Louis's power by promising in the secret Treaty of Dover to declare himself a Catholic, a fact that explained the connivance at recruiting for the British regiments in the French service, which caused a good deal of annoyance in the Commons. Danby's pressure on the king to make some concession to the prevalent anti-French feeling did lead to Charles consenting, in November 1677, to the marriage of William to the 15-year-old Princess Mary.

The third 'dynastic accident' of the reign was that no child resulted from the marriage of William and Mary. The birth of a child in the next few years would have influenced the politics of the Exclusion crisis by increasing the chance of the creation of a new Anglo-Dutch dynasty and so strengthening William's position. There is no means of knowing when William realized that he was to have no family, but clearly it was before 1688. The choice of the nonentity Prince George of Denmark to marry Mary's younger sister Anne in 1683 can hardly be described as accidental; his political insignificance was none the less a factor in the situation, as was the circumstance that, in spite of Anne's repeated pregnancies, no child survived infancy before the birth of the Duke of Gloucester in 1689.

For a time, when to Charles's dismay Louis refused to accept his proposals for a peace settlement and he had no choice but to follow the marriage of William and Mary with an Anglo-Dutch treaty in January 1678, there seemed a real possibility that England would intervene in the continental war. But Charles was reluctant to risk this – certainly without a previous grant of money from the House of Commons – and the House of Commons, in spite of a widespread hostility to France, was reluctant to vote money without a previous declaration of war. Without this, the Dutch made the Treaty of Nijmegen with Louis XIV, and the war which had caused Charles embarrassment came to an end.

In the autumn of 1678, therefore, the English troops which Charles had raised for his suggested intervention were still in being, pending a vote of money for their disbandment, and the more suspicious members of the opposition were wondering to what use they might be put within England. At the same time, Danby's known use of pensions seemed to be building up a Court Party in the Commons, and the Country Party had little hope of achieving anything positive there or of seeing the dissolution and general election for which Shaftesbury had striven (even contemplating for the purpose a temporary tactical alliance with James, who was equally hostile to Danby). There seemed to be no reason why the Cavalier Parliament should not last as long as the reign, or why that reign should not be followed by that of the dreaded Popish successor.

It was in a mood approaching desperation, therefore, that after some members of the Country Party had contacted Barrillon, the representative of a hated foreign power, they were suddenly given an unexpected opportunity in the excitement caused by the stories of Titus Oates and the mysterious death of the magistrate who had taken his depositions, Sir Edmund Berry Godfrey. They had no alternative to a policy of making every use of these unlooked-for circumstances.

IV

The fourth period of the reign, 1678–81, takes its whole colour from the stories of Titus Oates, one of the most discreditable figures in English history, of a supposed Popish Plot to murder the king. Originally, however, Oates's hopes were of clerical preferment through Danby, for the government had far greater patronage at its disposal

67

to reward informers than the opposition, and the opposition feared that it was all a trick to enable Danby to keep his armed forces on foot. Oates's original talk reflected upon many Catholics, but not upon James himself, who would be murdered as well as his brother, if he did not answer Papist expectations; Catholics themselves blamed Danby for launching the plot in the first place. If Danby was not at first averse to turning Oates's story to political advantage, he was overwhelmed in the panic after the death of Godfrey and the feeling that the government was not investigating the matter thoroughly enough; and Shaftesbury, the acknowledged leader of the opposition after his stay in the Tower for twelve months in 1677–8, was able to return to London, following three months' absence, and take charge of the agitation. Once he had done this, and Oates had turned to the opposition, Shaftesbury inevitably found himself in a position where he had to appear to give credence to any informer who came forward in support of Oates's story and kept the pot boiling.

To modern eyes, looking dispassionately at the stories of a supposed plot to murder the king by poisoning, stabbing or shooting him with a silver bullet, it is natural to suppose that any honest man would have seen through the lies and inconsistencies in a moment. But Charles's own privy councillors were not so sure; techniques for investigation were rudimentary and the facilities at the government's disposal for it were limited; modern rules of evidence and the need for corroboration of the stories of accomplices were not current; Oates was a particularly skilful and brazen liar, and people who did not know Oates's past record believed statements solemnly made on oath. Perhaps most important, the general public at first knew only the gist of his story and had no means of weighing the details of the evidence until people had made up their minds. There seems in all ages to be a propensity to believe in stories of conspiracies, or to say that there must be 'something in it', even if the whole could not be believed.

The result was comparatively small in terms of the

statute-book. Two Bills which the Country Party had long sought to enact at last passed all their stages and received the royal assent, but of these the Test Act, though it excluded Catholics from both Houses of Parliament until the time of George IV, had a proviso attached to it exempting James. To Shaftesbury's fury, this was carried by a small majority (variously reported) in the Lords and by only two votes in the Commons. The Habeas Corpus Amendment Act, which, it seems, passed the Lords only because the teller counted a fat peer as ten, restricted the government's potential powers of arbitrary imprisonment. Attempts have been made to argue that this was only a matter of stopping up technical loopholes and was thus of limited importance; but the fact that James later wanted to repeal it, and the government of William III actually suspended it, suggests that the traditional view of the Act is largely correct.

The difficulty of passing these Acts and obtaining the assent of Lords and king as well as Commons may have been one reason why the Whigs preferred to try to settle the central question of the succession by the drastic measure of exclusion, rather than by a series of Acts restricting the prerogative of a Popish successor. In the months after Oates had come forward, Charles offered to consent to 'whatsoever reasonable Bills you shall present . . . to make you safe in the reign of any successor', provided that they did not alter the line of succession or restrain either his own power or that of a Protestant successor. In the following April, he made this more concrete by offering to agree to laws preventing a Popish successor from making ecclesiastical appointments and from making or removing privy councillors without the consent of Parliament, thus dividing the opposition, for Halifax believed these 'limitations' to be feasible, whereas the main body of the Whigs did not. Although on the disintegration of Danby's party in the Commons the Cavalier Parliament was at last dissolved and was followed successively by three others, in which the Lower House had strong Whig majorities, their inability to press charges of impeachment against Danby showed that they could not rely on the Lords, and there was always the possibility that the king could evade any legislative programme by either prorogation or dissolution.

The Whigs therefore staked everything upon passing one short Bill, an Exclusion Bill, first presented to the Parliament of 1679, when it is noteworthy that some previously zealous leaders of the Country Party did not vote for it: they had been 'overtaken on the left'. For the purpose, they had to rely upon keeping the No-Popery passions at fever-heat and maintaining the pressure of Commons and people upon the king and his relatively inexperienced ministers, Sunderland, Halifax and Hyde. Of course the need for the Bill would have been obviated if Charles had agreed to back a Bill for his divorce from Catherine, a possibility revived by Shaftesbury as late as November 1680. In default of this, Monmouth's willingness to drop his old court connections and yield to the temptation of his own eventual advancement, backed by a number of adventurers who had their own prospects as well as the Protestant cause in mind, made him the Protestant hero. Shaftesbury was prepared to use this popularity, although he had previously written him off as part of the Court to which he was opposed.

Three times Charles's own ministers persuaded him to exile James, thus evading at once the pressures upon him and James's own importunities. The situation was exacerbated by Charles's illness in August 1679. Until then it had been possible for the hesitant to calculate that Charles might possibly outlive his brother, for there was only three years between them, and there was no reason to believe that (unless he was assassinated) his death was imminent. But now the matter was urgent; yet the newly elected Parliament was promptly prorogued and, in spite of the widespread petitioning movement, was not allowed to meet for another twelve months, so that neither exclusion nor Charles's proposed constitutional limitations on a Popish successor could be enacted. Not only did James return from exile during the recess, but in 1680 Exclusionists were systematically purged from the commissions of the peace and the deputy lieutenancies, so that all became aware of the consequences of opposition, in terms of local position, status and reputation, in this reign and the next. In the interim, Shaftesbury strove to keep the pot boiling by arranging for new Irish witnesses of a Popish Plot, and for the sensational presentation of James as a recusant and the Duchess of Portsmouth as a 'public nuisance' (that is, a prostitute). Although the government managed to evade this, it was made clear that when Parliament did meet, the excitement would be all the greater.

Some former leaders of the Country Party who had failed to vote for the first Exclusion Bill in the previous year became Exclusionists in 1680. Moreover, some of the king's own ministers, notably Sunderland, came to favour it; whether in the interests of William of Orange or from motives of self-preservation, they sought to co-operate with what they saw as inevitable. On previous occasions Charles had yielded to pressure. He had dismissed his long-standing minister, Clarendon; he had revoked the Declaration of Indulgence and abandoned his war with the Dutch; he had in the end dissolved the Cavalier Parliament and dismissed Danby as well. James was again sent into exile and was no longer at hand to stiffen his resolve.

Yet when it came to the point Charles did not weaken, and by making his opposition to the exclusion of his brother absolutely clear, he directly encouraged the House of Lords to throw the Bill out by a decisive majority on the very first reading. He further showed his determination by ending Parliament, dismissing Sunderland and calling the next Parliament to Oxford, where it would be away from the popular excitement in London and its members unable to prolong the session in the City, should they wish to resist another dissolution. A short session was generally expected, even by the Whigs, but Parliament was allowed to meet for only a week. Unlike his father, Charles had not given up his royal prerogative to prorogue and dissolve Parliament

71

without its own consent, and expectations that, if only for financial reasons, he would have to call another session in the autumn were disappointed. Court had triumphed over Parliament (or at least the majority in the Commons) and people.

There was to be no further Parliament in the remainder of the reign. Here we come to the last of the dynastic accidents that affected the fortunes of the Stuarts and the politics of the reigns of Charles and James. It has been pointed out already that in age there was only three years between the two brothers. If, instead of Charles dying at 54 and James at almost 68, the position had been reversed, English political and constitutional history would certainly have been modified; perhaps the history of Europe might have been different too, in that William III might not have been able to bring England into a coalition against Louis XIV in 1689. As it was, the personal government of Charles II lasted for only four years.

(Charles)
To 1684/85 — James to 1701

5 The Personal Government of Charles II

I have suggested elsewhere that the measure of success Charles enjoyed at the end of his reign came as the result of opportunism, rather than as a result of a systematically planned attempt to exalt his own authority at the expense of Parliament. Even his success in riding out the excitements of the Popish Plot crisis was not the result of Machiavellian tactics clearly formulated at the outset. It resulted from his ability to make use of circumstances as they offered themselves, and, for instance, to avail himself of the aid of people such as Halifax, and to take advantage of the failure of William of Orange to intervene.

There was, however, one basic fact which enabled Charles first to dissolve the successive Exclusion Parliaments and then to rule without summoning another, and this was the improvement which took place in his financial position and which made another Parliament unnecessary. It used to be thought that it was the renewed agreement with France for the provision of a subsidy in March 1681 that made his personal government possible, but when the figures are studied carefully it turns out that the sum provided by Louis was only marginal, and it ended in 1684. It provided an extra insurance against insolvency, but it did not turn a deficit into a surplus. The Commons has been accused of failing to vote taxation to meet the target figure of £1.2 million per year, which had been recognized in 1660 to be needed for the king's peacetime administration, thus producing the financial difficulties of the first half of the reign and the need to appeal to Louis (although Professor Chandaman, in his authoritative study of the public revenues (1975), argues that the taxes voted should have been adequate). But in the second half of the reign revenue had picked up in a way that no one had expected. To some extent this was the result of improved customs duties, when England was able to profit from neutrality in the continental war of 1674–8. Charles had not planned this – quite the contrary – and the decision in 1671 to collect the customs directly rather than employing syndicates of financiers to undertake it had been accidental, not planned; none the less, there was a considerable rise in yield. Falling back in the crisis years of 1678–81, it was resumed thereafter, and was accompanied by a return to direct control of the excise and hearth tax. The counterpart was a determined policy of retrenchment of expenditure, conducted by the Earl of Rochester with, for almost the first time in the reign, the support of the king; the abandonment of the expensive garrison of Tangier was only the most striking illustration of the economies. Professor Chandaman's conclusion is that in the last years of the reign the government's total net income was running at a rate substantially in excess of £1.4 million per annum, whereas, apart from the expenditure of the French subsidy of £125,000 per annum of which we have no details, expenditure during the last years of the reign did not exceed an average of roughly £1,175,000 per annum. The government's debts were reduced rather than liquidated, but then all governments of the day, including the States of Holland, had debts, and what mattered was government credit, which was far better in 1685 than it had been at the time of the Stop of the Exchequer.

Thus an opposition belief that Charles would soon be driven back on Parliament by his financial needs was disappointed. In one way his achievement was brittle, for like the ship-money regime of Charles I it was vulnerable to any emergency. Essentially he could not afford a foreign policy; he was sensitive to the danger that a renewal of Louis XIV's attempts to conquer Flanders would revive the belief, even among many Tories, that its preservation was an essential English interest. But in the years 1678–88 Louis contented himself with his gains at the Treaty of Nijmegen and from the *chambres de réunion*, together with the conquest of Luxemburg. This state of affairs was not likely to be permanent, but for the time being Charles had no need to take any initiative in foreign affairs and, taught by previous experience, was disinclined to do so unless it was absolutely unavoidable. As for Scotland and Ireland, whose rebellions had undermined his father, they were the least of Charles II's worries. The former, whose Bishops' Wars had brought about the recall of Parliament, was firmly and brutally repressed; this time the Covenanter rebellion was easily put down in 1679, James's vindictiveness shown, and according to Ogg (1934), the following years even saw a 'reign of terror'. As for Ireland, it gave no hint of a repetition of the events of 1641.

No matter how strong the financial position of the government, it could not have ruled successfully if a reluctant England had been seething with discontent or the gentry had refused to co-operate in enforcing its authority in the countryside. This was not the case. That there was some reaction in the government's favour is undoubted, even though its extent is difficult to evaluate. The government encouraged a flow of Tory addresses in support of the king's dissolution of Parliament from many of the same communities that had petitioned him to allow Parliament to meet eighteen months earlier. There was bound to be a reaction against the Popish Plot witnesses as soon as people had time to reflect on the weaknesses of their evidence, and to make matters worse some entered the pay of the government, and were unhesitatingly used against their former employers. Already in November 1682, L'Estrange's news-sheet, the *Observator*, turned from attacking Whigs and Dissenters to assault the 'Trimmers', who had favoured a 'middle way' between the parties. When, in 1683, following Shaftesbury's flight and death in exile, the government was able to publicize the story of the Rye House conspirators' plot to assassinate the king as well as James on their return from Newmarket, and to tie to this an alleged plot for a Whig rebellion, the revulsion went much further. For whatever the justification for taking legal action against James, there could be far less justification for violence against the undoubted rightful monarch, and the spectre conjured up by the Tory slogan of ' '41 is come again' presented itself. It was no wonder that corporations sent in further addresses of loyalty to the king. They were only partly explicable by the current threat to their charters.

Nevertheless there is probably some significance in the fact that Charles did not submit the popularity of his government to the test of another general election. It is likely that when he had arranged the French subsidy in March 1681, he had promised Louis not to call another Parliament after the Oxford one, but that subsidy lapsed after three years, and the Triennial Act required him to call Parliament after an interval of three years. Indolence may have had something to do with it, but the fact was that in spite of the reaction in his favour he was not prepared to take the chance.

Further, control over the elections of sheriffs and the Lord Mayor in London in 1682 was only achieved by manipulation and not the democratic decision of a majority of those entitled to vote. The uncertainties of the situation were sufficient to make Charles dependent upon the co-operation of Tories in the countryside, in the City and the municipal corporations. The immense patronage at the king's disposal gave him considerable advantages, but he had neither the bureaucracy nor the army to free himself from the need for their support. He could pack the judicial bench with lawyers like Jeffreys, control the appointment of London juries through suitable sheriffs, purge the corporations of Whig opponents through the *quo warranto* procedure against borough charters, see that the justices of the peace

76

and deputy lieutenants were Tories, and exercise a closer control of the Press than ever before in practice, but he could not call himself 'absolute'.

Therefore he took care not to break any other statutes apart from the solitary exception of the Triennial Act. He made no attempt to revive the Declaration of Indulgence for the benefit of his Catholic friends, and did not allow Catholic worship in public. He did not, like his successor, attempt to dispense Catholics from the provisions of the Test Act, although admittedly in practice James once more had the powers, but not the title, of Lord High Admiral. He did not attempt illegal exactions to improve his financial position. He allowed Danby to languish in the Tower under the Commons' charge of impeachment until 1684, when he was bailed, but not restored to office.

He had in fact to pursue Tory policies of legality and devotion to the Church of England, rather than relying solely on the willingness of courtiers and office-holders to do his bidding. He appealed to Tory and Anglican susceptibilities by instituting a persecution of Dissenters at least as severe as those of 1664–5, 1670 and 1675, and more long-lasting; this was their reward for taking part in Exclusionist politics. In return, Tories rallied loyally to their king, and the doctrine of non-resistance to the divinely appointed monarch resounded from all Anglican pulpits. The concluding years of the reign were not characterized by much freedom or diversity of thought.

This did not mean, however, that Tories necessarily supported a constitution without Parliament, or would co-operate actively in any policy that the king laid down. Just as some later Cavaliers welcomed the summoning of Parliament in 1640, after the personal government of Charles I, so it seems unlikely that all Tories (let alone Trimmers like Halifax) would have contented themselves without another meeting; the parliamentary tradition was too deeply rooted for that. And just as the Cavalier House of Commons of 1661 had turned into a house of critics by 1667, so the Tory Parliament of 1685, even though it was based on the remodelled municipal corporations, would not readily fall into a position of complete subservience. Although the wishes of some members to limit the revenue grant to James to a period of three years, instead of bestowing it for life, in order that 'Parliaments might be consulted the oftener' were not persisted in, by the autumn James was once more proroguing the assembly in reaction to an unfavourable vote.

Implicitly, therefore, the situation in 1685 remained uncertain and the constitutional balance between Court, Parliament and people still had to be decided. We cannot be sure what would have happened had Charles lived on, instead of dying at 54, and been able to avoid calling Parliament for a long period. Habits of obedience, the immense pull of royal patronage, the development of admistrative efficiency and the government's grip on the Press, pulpit and public expression of opinion might have reinforced the same trends that strengthened authoritarian rule in most of the Continent. On the other hand, the government still faced unresolved problems, and, while this is always true of all governments, they were important ones.

The ministers themselves were not united. Halifax, Rochester and Sunderland had quite different political records and outlooks, and Charles was as disinclined to resolve these undecided rivalries and to impose one unified policy as he had always been. All favoured the succession of James, but their attitudes to this prospect did not coincide. It was Monmouth's turn to be in exile while James returned to court (after narrowly avoiding shipwreck) in 1682, but there were still rumours that Monmouth, for whom Charles was known to cherish a certain fondness, would be allowed to return and even that James might once again have to return to Scotland as Lord High Commissioner. It is futile to spectulate how the situation might have developed, had not Charles died in 1685 and James's policies produced in 1688–9 the exclusion that the Whigs had vainly attempted to bring about in 1679–81.

78

It used to be thought that Locke's *Two Treatises of Government*, which were published at the end of 1689, were written to justify the Revolution, but it now seems to be clear that they were written from a version prepared in the earlier period. Locke was certainly closely associated by contemporaries with Shaftesbury, in whose household he had lived, and in 1683 he fled to Holland to escape the ruin of the Whigs. His *Two Treatises* were in any case the product of his reflections on his experience of the politics of the whole of his lifetime, just as the *Letter Concerning Toleration* of 1689 answered to his observations of intolerance; they were not mere abstract theoretical concoctions. His attention had been directed to the problem of whether resistance to authority was justified (in State as well as in Church) in 1675, when Danby's Test Bill had endeavoured to exclude from office and Parliament all who would not undertake not to attempt any alteration of the government as established in Church or State, and would not swear an oath against the lawfulness of resistance to royal authority. The *Letter from a Person of Quality* describing the debates on this test in the Lords may well have been written by Locke, who departed hurriedly for the south of France just after the pamphlet had been condemned to be burnt by the hangman. We know little of what he did while he was in France, but it seems to me not impossible that it was then, after his period in the Shaftesbury household from 1667–75, that he tried to formulate some of the ideas which later matured in a modified form in the *Two Treatises*.

Be that as it may, in 1685 Locke was in exile, the party of his former Whig friends was in ruins, and its remnants were muzzled and helpless to undertake any constitutional course of action. After the failure of Monmouth to overthrow the new monarch by force, it would be for James to destroy by his policies the position which had been built up in the reign of his brother; and for William by his intervention to revive the role of Parliament and 'people' (at least in the conventional Whig sense) in political life.

Guide to Further Reading

For detailed use there are two bibliographies to which reference may be made: M. F. Keeler, *Bibliography of British History: Stuart Period, 1603–1714* (1970) and W. L. Sachse, *Restoration England, 1660–1689* (1971), and there is a convenient short bibliography, including some more modern works, in J. R. Jones, *Country and Court: England, 1658–1714* (1978). J. S. Morrill's *Seventeenth-Century Britain, 1603–1714* (1980), though briefer than Keeler or Sachse, has comments which are especially useful to the student. This book therefore provides only a select reading list. General surveys of the whole Stuart period are excluded, and articles and mongraphs given in the reference list are not repeated here. Places of publication are in Great Britain unless otherwise indicated.

Sources and reference works

Here the indispensable work is A. Browning (ed.), *English Historical Documents, vol. VIII, 1660–1714* (1953), which contains not only documents, but many other aids to the student, including useful bibliographies, valuable and concise introductory surveys, maps and diagrams. A shorter selection is to be found in J. P. Kenyon, *The Stuart Constitution* (1966; revised edition in preparation) and there are extracts from both primary and secondary works in Joan Thirsk, *The Restoration* (Problems and Perspectives in History series, 1976); the latter, however, relates primarily to 1660 rather than to the whole reign. The three volumes of *The History of Parliament, 1660–1690*, edited by B. D. Henning (1983) contain a mass of biographical information about members, their families and constituencies which awaits digestion. This will be a lengthy process, but the volumes ought to be a great stimulus to researchers. It is to be hoped that as a more brilliant light is thrown on the world of Westminster, the world of Whitehall will not be neglected: a study of the Court is badly needed.

General

In many ways the easiest approach to the period as a whole is still through D. Ogg, *England in the Reign of Charles II*, 2 vols (originally published 1934; revised edition 1955), whose slightly Whiggish prejudices may easily be discounted, although obviously this then needs supplementing from more recently written works. There are no other books surveying the reign as a whole, unless one counts Burnet's contemporary *History of My Own Time: the reign of Charles the Second*, edited by O. Airy, 2 vols (1897), but *The Restored Monarchy, 1660–1688*, edited by J. R. Jones (1979) contains a collection of essays on some central themes. D. T. Witcombe, *Charles II and the Cavalier House of Commons, 1663–74* (1966); K. H. D. Haley, *William of Orange and the English Opposition, 1672–74* (1953); J. R. Jones, *The First Whigs* (1961); and J. P. Kenyon, *The Popish Plot* (1970) between them might be said to amount to a political survey of most of the reign, particularly when taken in conjunction with the opening chapters of J. R. Western, *Monarchy and Revolution: the English State in the 1680s* (1972), one of the few books surveying the decade as a whole. John Miller, 'Charles II and his Parliament', in *Transactions of the Royal Historical Society* 5th series, vol. 32 (1982) is an important article. A further article by Dr Miller appeared while this book was in the press: 'The Potential for "Absolutism" in Later Stuart England', *History*, vol. 69 (1984).

Biographies

Books on Charles II continue to appear in sizes ranging from my own Historical Association pamphlet (24 pp.) to M. Ashley, *Charles II: the Man and the Statesman* (1971, 358 pp.) and Antonia Fraser, *King Charles II* (1979, 500 pp.); R. Ollard, *The Image of the King: Charles I and Charles II* (1979) contains some useful insights. But there is none as good as John Miller's book on Charles's brother, *James II: A Study in Kingship* (1978). A good scholarly book on Clarendon, and, for that matter, an annotated edition of his autobiographical *Life*, are still lacking. Among the works on major statesmen are A. Browning, *Thomas Osborne, Earl of Danby*, 3 vols (1944–51), which is likely to remain definitive; K. H. D. Haley, *The First Earl of Shaftesbury* (1968); J. P. Kenyon, *Robert Spencer, Earl of Sunderland* (1958). There are no important recent books on other members of the Cabal, but a chapter on each in turn will be found in M. Lee, *The Cabal* (Urbana, Illinois, 1965).

Finance and administration

C. D. Chandaman, *The English Public Revenue, 1660–1688* (1975) is the outstanding work on this topic, which is basic to the understanding of the reign. It may be supplemented from two books which have a biographical cast to their titles, but throw light on the financial problems of the reign: D. C. Coleman, *Sir John Banks, Baronet and Businessman: A Study of Business, Politics and Society in Later Stuart England* (1963) and Christopher Clay, *Public Finance and Private Wealth: The Career of Sir Stephen Fox, 1627–1716* (1978). The opening of H. Roseveare, *The Treasury: The Evolution of a British Institution* (1969); H. Tomlinson, *Guns and Government: The Ordnance Office under the later Stuarts* (1979); and J. Childs, *The Army of Charles II* (1976) all relate to administrative topics.

Religion

Noteworthy books on religion over the whole period are G. R. Cragg, *Puritanism in the Period of the Great Persecution, 1660–1688* (1957); D. R. Lacey, *Dissent and Parliamentary Politics in England, 1661–1689* (New Brunswick, NJ, 1969); and John Miller, *Popery and Politics in England, 1660–1688* (1973). To my mind no account of the political side of the settlement of the Church at the Restoration is yet definitive, but for conflicting interpretations see R. S. Bosher, *The Making of the Restoration Settlement* (1951); G. R. Abernathy, 'The English Presbyterians and the Stuart Restoration, 1648–1663', *Transactions of the American Philosphical Society* (Philadelphia, 1965); and I. M. Green, *The Re-Establishment of the Church of England, 1660–1663* (1970). There are some useful articles in *From Uniformity to Unity, 1662–1962*, edited by G. F. Nuttall and O. Chadwick (1962).

Foreign policy

Specialist books on foreign policy are few; it can never be satisfactorily divorced from politics. K. Feiling, *British Foreign Policy, 1660–1672* (1930) is the only connected book on the first half of the reign, but rather difficult in style and detail for the reader unfamiliar with the period. Charles Wilson, *Profit and Power* (1957) deals with the Dutch war of 1665–7, but not that of 1672–4. On the second half of the period, there is no connected study, but there are two articles on the crisis of 1677–8, both published in the *English Historical Review:* K. H. D. Haley, 'The Anglo-Dutch Rapprochement of 1677', vol. LXXIII (1958) and C. L. Grose, 'The Anglo-Dutch alliance of 1678', vol. XXXIX (1924).

References

Places of publication are in Great Britain unless otherwise indicated.

Allen, D. 1976: Political clubs in Restoration London. *Historical Journal*, vol. xix

Browning, A. 1948: Parties and party organization in the reign of Charles II. *Transactions of the Royal Historical Society*, xix. 21–36

Browning, A. 1944–1951: *Thomas Osborne, Earl of Danby*, 3 vols

Browning, A. (ed.) 1953: *English Historical Documents, vol. VIII: 1660–1714*

Chandaman, C. D. 1975: *The English Public Revenue, 1660–1688*

Christie, W. B. (ed.) 1874: *Letters to Sir Joseph Williamson*, Camden Society

Clarendon, 1st Earl of. 1827: *Life of Edward, Earl of Clarendon*, 3 vols

Courtenay, R. P. 1836: *Memoirs of the Life, Works and Correspondence of Sir William Temple, Bart.*

Evans, J. T. 1979: *Seventeenth-century Norwich*

Grey, A. 1763: *Debates of the House of Commons, 1667–94*, 10 vols

Habakkuk, H. J. 1965: Landowners and the Civil War. *Economic History Review*, 2nd ser, xviii. 130–51

Haley, K. H. D. 1953: *William of Orange and the English Opposition, 1672–74*

Haley, K. H. D. 1968: *The First Earl of Shaftesbury*

Haley, K. H. D. 1970: Shaftesbury's lists of the lay peers and members of the Commons, 1677–8. *Bulletin of the Institute of Historical Research*, xliii. 86–105

Haley, K. H. D. 1983: *Charles II*. Historical Association pamphlet. First edition 1963

Halifax, 1st Marquis of. 1969 edn: *Complete Works*, edited by J. P. Kenyon

84

Henning, B. D. (ed.), 1940: *The Parliamentary Diary of Sir Edward Dering, 1670–3*, New Haven, Conn.

Henning, B. D. (ed.), 1983: *The History of Parliament, 1660–1690*, 3 vols

Holiday, P. G. 1970: Land sales and repurchases in Yorkshire after the Civil Wars, 1650–1670. *Northern History*, v. 67–92

Holmes, C. 1980: *Seventeenth-century Lincolnshire*

Jones, J. R. 1961: *The First Whigs*

Jones, J. R. 1978: *Country and Court: England, 1658–1714*

Locke, J. 1689: *Two Treatises of Government*

Locke, J. 1689: *Letter Concerning Toleration*

North, R. 1740: *Examen*

Ogg, D. 1934: *England in the Reign of Charles II*, 2 vols

Parliamentary History, 1806–20, ed. W. Cobbett, 36 vols (Quotations are from vol. iv)

Plumb, J. 1967: *The Growth of Political Stability in England, 1675–1725*

Thirsk, J. 1954: The Restoration land settlement. *Journal of Modern History*, xxvi. 315–28

Index